Video Games & Your Kids

Video Games & Your Kids

How Parents Stay in Control

Hilarie Cash, PhD
and
Kim McDaniel, MA

Idyll Arbor, Enumclaw, WA

A subsidiary of Idyll Arbor, Inc.

Editor: Ken Lucas

Library of Congress Cataloging-in-Publication Data

Cash, Hilarie, 1952-
  Video games & your kids : how parents stay in control / Hilarie Cash and Kim McDaniel.
      p. cm.
  Includes bibliographical references and index.
  ISBN 978-1-930461-05-5 (alk. paper)
  1. Video games and children--United States. 2. Video gamers--Psychology. I. McDaniel, Kim, 1963- II. Title. III. Title: Video games and your kids.
  HQ784.V53C37 2008
  649'.55--dc22
                                                                        2008013275
ISBN 9781930461055

For Luke, Erin, and Anna

Contents

Foreword

By Dr. Charles Fay
The Love and Logic Institute

Back in the old days…the nineties…I thought I was nuts.

Working with families across the nation, I was seeing ever increasing numbers of young people…and adults…who'd do just about anything for a fix. They seemed completely obsessed…hooked…addicted! Their drug of choice wasn't marijuana, crack, heroin, or alcohol. They weren't compulsive gamblers or sex addicts. Most of them came from relatively "normal" families like my own.

I found myself wondering, "It looks like addiction, but could it really be?"

They displayed all of the devastating signs of alcohol, drug, gambling, and other major dependencies…but I still wasn't sure. "Am I just nuts?" I pondered, "How could someone get addicted to the Internet or video games?"

Until I met the authors of this book, I thought I was alone in thinking that folks could develop *bona fide* addictions to the fast-paced, unpredictable fantasy lives provided by video games and hanging ten on the Web. I second-guessed myself. "Am I too old-fashioned? Maybe I don't understand. Am I too hard on kids and families these days? Maybe I'd better enter the 20th century and embrace the Cyber world."

Have you second-guessed yourself? Have you denied the fact that this cunning enemy has crept into your home? Has it sneaked up on your kids? Do any of them:

- o Seem more interested in electronic relationships than real ones?
- o Spend hours hunched in front of a screen?
- o Become extremely agitated...even aggressive...when they can't game, chat, or surf the Web?
- o Seem willing to lie, steal, cheat, and flunk out of school in order to spend more time with their computer and their Cyber friends?

There's great hope! That is, as long as we understand that the threat is real. As you turn the pages of this book, your eyes will open to the signs, symptoms, and tragic consequences of computer, Internet, and video-gaming addiction. Through real-life stories and examples, you'll learn that too much exposure, or the wrong type of exposure, puts our children at risk for developing:

- o Problems with attention, learning, and self-control
- o Impaired social skills
- o Emotional problems, such as anxiety, low self-esteem, and depression

o Aggression and an attitude of indifference to human pain and suffering

o Physical problems, such as obesity, eye strain, carpel tunnel syndrome, etc.

o An obsession with sex and pornography

If your goal is to protect your children from these sad consequences, you're making a wise investment in your child's future by reading this book. As you read, you'll also learn that love is the main ingredient of an addiction-free home. You'll also see that this love is multifaceted. One aspect involves loving our kids enough to set limits on video game and Internet use. Another involves loving them enough to supervise and pay close attention to what they are viewing or playing. Another dimension of this love is demonstrated by our willingness to hold them accountable for their misdeeds and their poor decisions while using their computers or video games. Of course, there's no substitute for the love communicated by time. Kids need lots of it. When we fill them up with our loving time, they have no need to find "Cyber love" on the Web.

For many, the hardest aspect of parental love involves slaying the dual dragons of denial and codependency. In this book, you'll gain the understanding required to spot these monsters. You'll learn why it's so important to destroy them, and you'll see that the most loving parents are those who aren't afraid to make their kids mad. Yes! Being willing to upset our kids now — so that they later live happy and responsible lives — is probably the highest level of love we can communicate. The pages of this book will give you the confidence to cradle your kids in this powerful form of affection.

Some of you are reading this book because computer or video-gaming addiction has already touched your family. You're hurting. In fact, you're hurting big time! Some of you may be hurting so badly that you've barely got the energy to read this page.

We all make mistakes as parents. Even so-called "parenting experts" such as me mess up! Even when we haven't made big child-rearing errors, our kids can still end up facing big problems. Regardless of why your child has developed an unhealthy dependency on the Internet or video games, feeling guilty or blaming yourself is counterproductive. It drains you of the energy required to take the steps outlined in this book. Give yourself a break...take a deep breath, and take to heart the information provided here. There's a brighter horizon out there, just as long as you are willing to let the following pages guide you toward it!

Thanks for loving your kids!
Dr. Charles Fay
The Love and Logic Institute

Preface

We all know that video games in moderation can be fun. But what we have tried to do in this book is to warn parents about the harmful and destructive effects that video games can have and are having on the lives and behavior of their kids.

If your child's behavior has you concerned, or is causing you to wonder, then this book is for you.

In the pages that follow are the stories of children and young people who have been seriously affected by video gaming. We have changed names to protect our client's identities, and some of the stories have been created out of several clinical histories.

South Korea and China have declared video game addiction their most pressing public health problem. Video game addiction is minimized in America, perhaps because it remains hidden within individual households. We do not have the widespread cultural phenomenon of Cyber cafes where gaming is conducted in public. Where this is the custom, the tragedies that occur are public as well.

The authors of this book are clinicians with years of clinical experience; our findings are based on that experience and, where available, scientific evidence. Scientific investigation in the field of video gaming is growing, but the field is young; the research is in its early stages. We are grateful to those whose findings we draw on for this book.

The psychiatric community is examining video game addiction and is considering its addition as a psychological disorder in the next version of its Diagnostic and Statistical Manual (DSM). In the meantime, young (and not-so-young) people are suffering and need help. It is our hope that this book will serve as a wake-up call and that it will give you the information and guidance you need to face one of the most perplexing challenges of parenting in the computer age.

Acknowledgements

There are many people who have supported and inspired this project. First among them are our families. Our children have given us a personal window into the world of video games, helping us understand their powerful draw. Our families have cheered us on and, in the case of Kim's wonderful husband, Rob, contributed materially to the content of this book.

Our clients are to be thanked next, for without their courageous work in our consult rooms, we would not fully understand the seriousness of the video game problem. Over the years there have been many children, teens, and adults who have sought our help. We have had to meet their challenge and learn much more than we ever knew before about video games and addiction; we feel honored to be a part of their healing process.

Hilarie wishes to thank Jay Parker, her colleague and professional partner, for all he has taught her about the nature of addiction, whether chemical or behavioral, the process of recovery, and for his unflagging good cheer, support, and wise counsel. She also thanks the many people who have understood the need for this book and have contributed, through lively discussion, and suggested reading, to the understandings that are embodied in this work.

Foremost among them is Hilarie's mother, Romni Cash, and her friends Sunny Ruthchild, Katarina Digman, and Bruce Wolcott. Her friends Jeannie and David Brooks provided much appreciated editorial help as well as encouragement. Jim Toone gave marvelously helpful editorial feedback, as did Ruth Fruland, Katarina Cernozubov-Digman, and Jerald Block.

Kim also wishes to express her gratitude to the many people who have contributed to the writing of this book. First and foremost to her husband Rob and daughters Erin and Anna for their patience and encouragement. Erin and Anna have certainly listened to their mother talk about gaming more than any teen would care to hear — which is saying a lot! She also wishes to express her deeply felt appreciation to her father, Jerry Saklad, who early on taught her the value of compassion that led her to pursue a career as a therapist.

Our thanks to professional colleagues Elaine Duncan, Mary Lee McElroy, Marilyn Germano, Melanie Gale, David Evans, Lief Tellman, Patrick Hart, Joy Rome, Jaylene Dunning, and Erica Baxter. The regular consult meetings in which they all engaged kept alive the passion to address this problem.

We thank Tom Blaschko of Idyll Arbor, Inc. for seeing the value of this book and Ken Lucas for his editorial assistance.

Introduction

Video games are now firmly embedded in the cultural identity of America's teenagers. As of the writing of this book (2008), it is now estimated that 90 percent of our youth are playing video games. They are using handheld devices or full-fledged, Internet-based, multiplayer games. Most are nonchalant about them, enjoying them as part of the many things they do for pleasurable entertainment, integrating them into their lives without harmful effect. Others, however, have grown so dependent on these games that they are abandoning their lives to pursue this activity, which they seem to prefer above all others.

How are parents responding? Many adults who have come of age in the video game era are quite comfortable allowing video games into their family life; adults who did not grow up with this technology vary in their responses to it. Some admire it and assume it is good for their children;

others mistrust it and feel at war with it (and with their children or grandchildren who want to play the games unfettered).

Our experience as therapists and as parents has taught us that, indeed, video games can be a benign part of a child's life as long as parents make sure their children are not playing too long or playing inappropriate games. We make recommendations in this book that, if followed, should successfully guide parents as they decide what games to allow and how much time to allow them. The good video games (ones that people enjoy playing) are based on solid learning principles. Because they are interactive (the player is an *active* participant rather than a *passive* observer), the well-designed games are powerful tools, allowing players to: 1) solve problems in increasingly complex ways; 2) try out new behaviors from which they can learn new things about themselves; and 3) engage in new experiences that give them a window into something completely outside the realm of their ordinary experience. Increasingly, the power of video games is capturing the interest of educators, who are designing games that will harness these same learning principles in compelling, pleasurable ways so that children in the classroom will learn the desired content of subject areas and the critical thinking skills that will make them competitive in today's high-tech world.

Our culture's relationship to video games is not all rosy, however. There are some serious problems with video games in particular and with the Internet in general which parents need to understand and address if they are to successfully shepherd their children into adulthood. Keeping our focus on video games for the purposes of this book, we discuss these potential problems.

As mentioned in our Preface, South Korea and China have declared video game addiction as their number one public health problem. Think about that for a moment. Why do we think of video gaming as the pinnacle of cool entertainment (and video game developers as stars), while it is seen by the authorities in those two countries as a terrible public health threat? Perhaps the reason has something to do with the private nature of video gaming in this country. In Asia, gaming is largely done in public. Here, it's done in private, which isolates each family with a problem and, perhaps, leads them to believe they have failed their child in some shameful way. After all, everyone else seems to be having a good time with this ultra-cool entertainment.

Where can they turn for help? There are precious few counselors who declare gaming as a specialty. Currently, there are no treatment programs for video game addiction except in Europe and Asia, which is too far away for most people to even hear about. So the problems that can develop with unlimited video game play are not talked about much, either at a national or private level. Parents feel alone with their family problem and do not know what to do.

This is why we wrote this book.

In the first chapter, we discuss the addictive nature of most video games, especially the most popular ones. The very principles that make games highly pleasurable can keep players so engrossed that they easily lose track of time, bodily needs, responsibilities, and even long-forgotten pleasures. Over time, physical dependency can develop. We provide readers with assessment tools, allowing them to determine whether there is a serious problem for a member of the family.

In the second chapter, we discuss how gaming to excess can change the very structure of the brain and cause harmful health effects, especially to a growing child whose brain and body are highly malleable. The skills developed through moderate gaming can be benign, but unlimited and unsupervised gaming can have negative effects on, among other things, attachment, academic abilities, social skills, mood, and physical health.

Chapter three is focused on how to set limits with your children to ensure that their gaming activities stay within healthy limits. This chapter will take you step by step through the process of identifying your family's needs and maintaining your boundaries. The concept of the "family meeting" as a communication tool is introduced. Guidelines are offered to help you use this important tool with success in your own home.

Children go through distinct developmental periods, each with its own challenges and windows of opportunity for growth. By taking a closer look at what each child needs at a specific developmental period, we can make better decisions about which games to allow into their lives and how much exposure should be permitted. In the chapters that follow we examine the influence that video and computer games have had on our children at five specific developmental periods: infants and toddlers (birth – age 2), early childhood (ages 2 – 6), elementary school years (ages 6 – 12), teenage years (ages 12 – adult), and the special case of adult children who are addicted to gaming and are living at home. These chapters are filled with real-life examples of children who have had problems associated with their gaming behavior, some mild and some severe. Each of these chapters features a section called "What Parents Can Do" which offers practical suggestions that we hope will empower all parents who are concerned about their child's emotional and psychosocial needs to take charge of the technology that is used in their homes.

The final chapter of this book (Chapter 9) is dedicated to helping families who know their child is a gaming addict and feel that it is too late to use our suggestions. Here we examine "The Formal Intervention

Option," and walk parents through the process. There are case studies and stories of how other families have handled this tragic problem, along with specific steps that parents can take to regain control of their homes and get needed help for their addicted child.

At the back there is a glossary of the sometimes-puzzling terms used on the Internet or in video gaming. If you feel lost in the world of video games, you might want to start your reading there. Knowledge of what is really going on is required before you can make changes.

1
What is Gaming Addiction?

It's two in the morning. Jason is full of nervous anticipation of the challenge and fun that lie just ahead. He's not tired, even though he has slept only three hours in the last two days. He already knows he won't get up for school when 6:15 rolls around. He might not sleep at all. It all depends on the success of his "mission." His *guild*[1] is camped out where they know a *boss*[2] is going to show up. They hope it will drop some rare armor when they defeat it that, they have agreed, will become the

---

[1] The group formed by multiple players, like a clan or team, to achieve a shared gaming goal.
[2] A powerful enemy in a game that must be fought and overcome for players to advance or earn points in a game.

property of Jason. With the power this armor bestows, he will be able to protect other members as they *level up*[3]. He'll attain serious prestige in this game fairly soon...if all goes as hoped.

School holds no interest for Jason. It's boring. And his social life there sucks, too. He hasn't found anyone who likes to game like he does, and the games other kids are into are as boring as they are. That is *not* how he feels about his on-line friends. Time spent with them is never boring. They have important things to do in the game. They love each other; they would lay down their lives for each other.

There is a girl in the guild that he really likes, too. They've chatted privately quite a bit. She is two years older and that is fine with him. If he can get some money together, he'll go visit her in California. There is definitely romance between them. Jason is in love; he's sure she is, too. He has asked his parents to send him there for a visit and they have refused. He hates them for their stinginess and lack of understanding. He knows he'll flunk out of school soon and is glad. He would love to see how upset his parents will be, especially his dad. And it will be a relief to get it over with. He's pretty sure his parents won't kick him out of the home; they will be too worried about their *little boy*. That will leave him free to play as he likes and not be hassled by his parents beyond the occasional lecture, yelling, and tears that he knows will come, then pass.

Upstairs, Jason's mother awakens and heads toward the bathroom. She pauses by the stairs and listens. She can hear her son talking into his headset, the sound muffled by distance and a closed bedroom door. A wave of despair and depression sweeps over her. What is going to happen to her son? Can her marriage survive the strain? Her husband

---

[3] Increase skill and power by getting a character to a higher level. Characters start at level one and increase their level as they kill enemies, learn new skills, etc.

blames her for being too lenient with the boy; she blames him for being too harsh. He's angry all the time and never misses an opportunity to throw Jason a verbal barb. It must be devastating to Jason's self-esteem. How can they protect their young daughter from the toxic atmosphere that now pervades the house? She has run out of ideas. It feels to her as if she's watching a train wreck that is happening in slow motion and that she is powerless to stop.

Jason's father wakes up, his body missing the warmth of his wife. He knows immediately that she is listening to their son gaming and grows angry. It will be a while before he's able to sleep again, and this makes him angrier. As he lies in the dark waiting for his wife to return, he thinks about the mess they are all in. He can see so plainly that his son is on a path to nowhere, that he will never be successful in the adult world if he doesn't change course. His wife sees it, too, but she is weak and resists taking strong action with the boy. Jason needs to be kicked out of the house if he fails school, which seems inevitable. *Tough love* they call it. He believes in it, but his wife does not. She wants help for Jason; he wants to give Jason a good swift kick in the pants.

He bridles at the notion that he is somehow to blame for the mess Jason's in. It's a father's job to be the disciplinarian and instill values of hard work. It's not his job to be a nurturer. That's for women who are good at it. Compared to his own father, he's a saint. He has never hit the boy, only yelled at him when he needed it. He does not understand why his son seems to hate him so much. He thinks it must be anger over their recent move, done for his career, combined with the negative influences of that Internet world his son now inhabits. His son is addicted, no doubt about it. The one time they tried to remove the computer from Jason's room he threatened suicide. They believed him. He looked completely crazy, so they gave back the computer and breathed a sigh of relief when

Jason returned to his normal, withdrawn demeanor; happy when gaming, angry at any interference from parents.

◊ ◊ ◊

Stories like this are played out around the world every day. Jason is sixteen, but he could be younger or older. When Jason's parents finally contacted us, his addiction was so entrenched that a formal intervention was necessary. They contacted an intervention specialist who was familiar with video game addiction. The interventionist gathered family and friends, figured out what they all wanted to say to Jason, and made a plan for what would happen immediately following the intervention. The intervention took place, Jason went to Outward Bound (a wilderness program) for three weeks and when he returned home he had no Internet access. He attended group, family, and individual therapy and today is finishing high school. The authors don't know how his life's story will unfold, of course. We just hope he is learning how to succeed in the real world. If he can do that, then maybe he will be able to play video games in a way that doesn't throw his life out of balance. However, it is possible that, like an alcoholic, he must *abstain* from the games that he most enjoys if he is truly *powerless* over them.

Hilarie, one of the authors of this book, has a sixteen-year-old son who loves video games. He once regretted that he had a mother who refused to let him play on-line games in the home. She can't control what he does when he visits his friends, and she knows he may play some of the massive multiplayer on-line role-play games (hereafter known as MMORPGs) in other homes. These are games in which thousands of players from around the world log onto the game and interact with each other. They generally form up into *guilds* to go on *quests*, accomplish various tasks and, over time, their *avatar* (the on-screen characters they have created) *levels up* (increases in skill and power). Hilarie's son likes plenty of other well known games that can be played either on-line or off. He likes a game about battling evil aliens that is a fast-paced, exciting, first-person *shooter* (you have the perspective of actually holding the weapon that you shoot). The virtual worlds and storylines of these games are appealing and we can easily understand why he finds them so fascinating.

So what is the problem? Why can't he own certain games? Why would he think his mother was being ridiculous, and why would his mother assume guilt for depriving him of the experiences that so many of his friends are having? Hilarie once worried that he wouldn't fit in with his peers and that he would resent her fairly strict stance. That was back when he was thirteen and fourteen. Now that he is sixteen, he never complains about it. He enjoys playing a soccer or football video game, either against the computer or against someone else, like his father. He does play other video games with his friends at their homes. He would say that these video games are a hobby of his, but if you asked him about his *true* hobbies, the first thing he would tell you about is his guitar. This is part of why she won't let him own some of the exciting games he enjoys. She is convinced that her son, who has a fairly shy nature, loves fantasy and easily gets obsessed with what interests him, could have ended up addicted to those types of games. He thinks so, too. Instead of gaming, he has poured himself into his music and now hopes to be a successful musician some day.

This outcome is really no surprise. Hilarie is a psychotherapist specializing in the problems of video game and Internet addiction. This is actually an unlikely specialty for her because, at one time, she knew little about computers and has only been personally interested in them as tools, not entertainment. However, when she first moved to Seattle in 1994 and started a private practice, a twenty-five-year-old client introduced her to the phenomenon of video game addiction. He came for therapy because he was depressed and his marriage was falling apart. As they worked together, it soon became apparent that he spent most of his waking hours playing an early on-line multiplayer game. He played it at work (and got fired twice because of it); he played it all evening; he played it instead of sleeping. Eventually he was able to curb his addictive behavior, but not before he lost his marriage.

She was fascinated by this client's experience and investigated further. Back then, there were very few people writing about the problem or doing research. But those who wrote confirmed her impression that video game play and the Internet, in general, could lead to an *addiction*. Her son was little then. Armed with the information she had about the power of video games and the Internet, she was a very cautious mom and still is. Her goal is to limit his time with video games and the Internet so that his brain and body can develop through a wide variety of normal, real-world experiences. Her concern is that if he spends unlimited time in front of screens, he will not develop into a well-balanced person, with the physical, intellectual, emotional, and social skills he'll need to be successful in his adult life.

Kim, this book's other author, is the mother of two teenaged daughters. She is also a psychotherapist, but her journey with her own children differed from that of Hilarie. Kim found that limiting screen time was rarely a problem with her daughters. Like many girls, they usually preferred interactive social activities with friends and family to using the computer or television. They played computer games, usually asking a family member to play with them. There were no warning signs of addictive behavior. For them a game was just a game. As they grew into their teenage years, on-line games were introduced and played with parental supervision. With parental support, they learned how to protect their on-line identity, as well as how to deal with bullies and unwanted sexual comments.

Sometimes they complained about the way female characters were depicted in these games, which led to rich family discussions about sexism and racism.

However, while gaming addiction was not a concern to her daughters, the safe use of Internet *social networks* was. There were many lively discussions about MySpace, Facebook and YouTube. And to ensure that the use of the social networking sites continued to be safe and supervised, the Internet was never allowed in their bedrooms. Instead, two computers were made available that sit side by side on a table in their family room. The girls enjoyed a limited level of privacy, always knowing that their parents were a few clicks away from monitoring their on-line activity.

There are many reasons why most parents are not as cautious as the co-authors of this book. Most simply do not know what the potential problems are. That is why this book has been written. In the pages that follow, you will read about some of the cases we have dealt with over the years. They illustrate what can happen if you do not take appropriate action to limit your child's video game time. We don't want to scare you. We don't want you to think of all video games as evil. We want you to have the information you need to make good choices about them.

Gamers are passionate about gaming. They usually do not see anything wrong with the amount of time they spend gaming and are quick to challenge anyone who questions it. All of this might leave you, the reader, conflicted. Perhaps you appreciate the intellectual challenges of many games, and appreciate the phenomenal artistry that goes into creating the fantasy worlds of these games. Perhaps you have sympathy for the private, social, on-line world your child inhabits. There are indeed many things to be admired about video games.

But video games also have the potential to harm your child's development. In this chapter we will share some of the information we have gathered over the years. We want you to understand what addiction is, how to recognize it, how to prevent it, and what to do if it is already a problem for your child. We will ask you to think about how you inadvertently may be allowing video games to become a problem for your family. If so, how can you change this?

In the following chapters, we will give you information about how excessive video game play can influence your child's development in damaging ways. We will also examine harmful health effects that can be caused by gaming. We will then explain the developmental stages that children go through, what they need at each stage, how video games fit into that picture, how you can set appropriate limits with your child, and how to create and maintain close bonds with your child in this age of video games.

A few case studies follow, illustrating the types of problems parents face:

Rob

Rob was eighteen years old when he voluntarily came for treatment. His mother agreed that he had a serious gaming habit and needed help. It was she who called and explained that her son had failed high school, failed his classes at the local community college, and it appeared as if he were about to fail again. He was bright, she said, but had a hard time socially. She was surprised that he had expressed an interest in getting help for his gaming addiction, but, of course, she was delighted. Her son had been gaming for about five years. At first he played console games, and then discovered multi-user Internet games. His social life was limited to occasional local-area network (LAN) parties (where gamers come together in one place with their computers, which they link together) and the live chatting he did from the privacy of his bedroom while gaming on-line. His grades had gone steadily downhill through high school, until he dropped out in his senior year.

This mother expressed love and concern for her son. She knew he was in deep trouble with his gaming, but nothing she had tried had succeeded in curbing his behavior. Even though he was now eighteen, and not doing anything productive with his time (no paid work and failing in school), the mother was unwilling to ask him to leave home fearing that he would come to harm if forced out.

He tried to cut back on his gaming many times, but always felt increasingly restless and irritable until he could stand it no more. Once he logged on and began playing, he found simple relief. As he played and became deeply engrossed in the game, he experienced enormous pleasure. He forgot about all his troubles: the schoolwork waiting to be done, the job needing to be found, and his upset mother who wanted him to "do something useful." He forgot about his lack of friends or a girlfriend as he engaged in lively on-line game-related chat.

Rob would become so deeply engrossed in the game that he lost all track of time. When his mother told him good night at 11 PM, he would ignore his own exhaustion and would play until three or four in the morning and thus miss another day of school. When he finally woke up, he would be upset with himself and resolve to get his homework done, even though it was way overdue. But he would find that he couldn't really concentrate on it. His mind was preoccupied with the game. He had some ideas about what he wanted to do with his character and he didn't want to be gone from the game for long. He needed to put in the long hours of play or he would risk losing the power and status that he had worked so hard to earn. Within an hour, Rob would be back on-line. And so it went.

When Rob entered treatment, he quickly admitted to gaming addictively. We spoke about his need to limit his gaming in order to have time to get his schoolwork done. We agreed that he should find ways to socialize with young people in the real world. We agreed that working might be a very good thing for him. We discussed treatment options, in particular the question of whether to taper off his game playing or embark on complete abstinence. He would not consider abstinence. But, week after week, Rob came in and reported that he had failed to limit himself to the gaming hours we had mutually agreed would move him in the right direction. Rob was told that he probably would need to abstain from gaming for a time in order to accomplish what he wanted. This would be difficult but not impossible, and we would build as much support into this as we could.

Rob discussed his problem and his choices over the course of several sessions. In the end, he left therapy because neither he nor his mother could face the prospect of giving up the safe cocoon that gaming had provided them. This story took place long before we had a formal intervention specialist to work with, before the creation of our gamers' support group, and before tools were available for parents to use in limiting game time on a computer. Today, we would consider recommending formal intervention to his mother, as well as individual and group therapy for both. We can't know if it would have worked, but it might have been worth a try.

Understanding Addictions

Addiction is any pleasurable behavior that renders a person unable to stop once started and which is pursued in spite of negative consequences. Over time, the individual develops a tolerance to a given level of the addictive activity or substance; he or she stops feeling satisfied at a certain level of use and requires more activity or substance to get the original euphoria. When unable to engage in the addiction, the person enters *withdrawal*. This means the addict experiences physical and emotional feelings that range from uncomfortable to miserable. The addict has lost control over her behavior. She might deny that she has lost control, but those who know the addict well can see it.

People once thought that it was possible to become addicted only to ingested substances such as alcohol or heroin. The idea of becoming addicted to a *behavior* seemed absurd, although in everyday life people spoke casually about being addicted to eating, love, or exercise. Today, we know that certain behaviors do elevate a neurochemical called *dopamine* and that this neurochemical is primarily responsible for producing an elevated mood. We all want to experience pleasure in our lives. We are designed to do so through ordinary, healthy activities, like singing to our babies, watching Sunday night football, making love to our spouses, having a drink after work with a buddy, pulling off a successful dinner party, strolling through a park, watching a funny movie, or listening to music. We can thank dopamine for our joyful feelings.

Research and experience have shown that certain behaviors can become addictive when they are particularly effective in boosting dopamine and can be artificially sustained. Gambling is a good example of this. Sex and romance can also be engaged in addictively. It is no surprise, therefore, that 12-step groups now exist to help those who have become addicted to these particular behaviors. Video game playing can also be addictive. It is such a recent phenomenon that very few 12-step programs address the problem. Over time this is sure to change.

Intermittent reinforcement is the term psychologists use to describe the strong satisfaction we all tend to feel when we do something that rewards us — but not every time, and not predictably. It is human nature to grow bored with things that are predictable.

For instance, once you have mastered a game and know that you will win every time you play (because you know exactly what moves need to be made), you tire of the game and turn to something else. This is perhaps the strongest reason why the best video games are so addictive. They reinforce *intermittently*, just as gambling does. The player enters a world full of challenges and feels rewarded for surmounting those challenges. In the most popular video games, there are infinite possibilities. When you play with other gamers (sometimes numbering in the thousands), there is no end to what you may be able to do that will be interesting and new. You can create and change your character, you can be several characters in several different games, you can join or leave others in the game at will, and you can decide who you are and what you want to do. Many people find this unlimited freedom and never-ending action quite intoxicating.

The fact that players can game *anonymously* is also rewarding. We all know that we enjoy the freedom of anonymity. Haven't you had the experience of talking more openly with a complete stranger than with your spouse? Game players are known in the game only by the character they present. The behavior of that character will have no consequences in the real world, so a player can do whatever he or she wishes without fear of consequences beyond the game. The freedom this engenders is, again, intoxicating.

There are a few other factors that play into the fast growth of video game misuse among children. One is the easy *accessibility* of computers and the Internet.

Many parents allow their children to have a computer with Internet access in their bedrooms. Console games are often found there as well. When gaming becomes so accessible, there is little to stop children from turning to the computer as a first choice when they are bored, lonely, and anxious. Since parents do not see what is going on, it is easy for a child to game instead of doing homework or sleeping. Even when families limit computers or a game console to a less private area of the home, easy access means potential trouble if content and time are not carefully supervised.

Affordability is also a factor in this social phenomenon. Computers, game consoles, and the games themselves are inexpensive enough that the vast majority of American households have one or both of them. The monthly fee for Internet access is affordable for most.

A Closer Look

Let's look more closely at video game play and a child's journey from normal, healthy play, through overuse, to addiction. In our experience (and confirmed by early research), a child with a healthy relationship to computers and video games spends, over the course of a week, fewer than two hours per day chatting and gaming. When a healthy child is not gaming, she or he is more likely to be engaging in solo, imaginative play, social play with other children, handling responsibilities like chores and homework, doing sports or other extra-curricular activities, and spending time with family. This general picture holds true, no matter what the age of the child.

If it were possible to look at this child's brain throughout the day with the sophisticated technology that exists, we would see normal brain patterns, with spikes of brain activity associated with certain real-world activities. Most notably, one would see the child's pleasure pathway unusually active during video game play. In the words of Dr. Daniel Amen, a psychiatrist and brain researcher, the brain is being *inflamed* by gaming. Is this a problem? Probably not, in limited doses (although we do not know that for sure). Dr. Amen and other professionals recommend no more than half an hour of such inflammatory stimulation. Different games demand somewhat different processes, but, extrapolating from what is known so far from research, all the popular games exert a tremendously stimulating influence on the brain. Dopamine is being released along with other chemicals, such as cortisol, and adrenaline. There is little direct evidence as yet, but at least one study has clearly demonstrated increased levels of dopamine during game play. There is also evidence that as arousal from gaming increases, some areas of the frontal lobes shut down (for how long, we do not yet know), while other areas of the brain become tremendously active. This means that as arousal (both pleasure and fight/flight) increases, judgment and decision-making decrease.

Your healthy child can, potentially, become an unhealthy child if he or she is allowed to spend more and more time gaming. Research suggests that once a child's gaming occupies more than two hours per day, that child has entered the slippery slope of misuse and, if allowed to continue, could slide into addiction. We will discuss the signs and symptoms of addiction a little later in this chapter.

Margaret

Margaret was a twelve-year-old who loved to play a life-simulation video game called The Sims. At home she was becoming noticeably more cranky and uncooperative when her parents set limits on her video gaming. She loved to play after dinner, and resented being reminded to do her homework. She argued that they should let her be in charge of her schedule, that she would get her work done, that they should stop worrying and stop bugging her. When bedtime arrived, she delayed and argued. Her parents, who were used to raising a fairly cooperative child, were unprepared to handle the new situation. They wondered if, perhaps, their daughter was correct. Perhaps she was old enough to be in charge and they should let her flounder a bit to figure it out on her own. After all, their daughter was almost a teenager and weren't all teenagers cranky? Didn't parents need to back off and allow their children to learn from their own mistakes? If they stopped battling over homework and bedtime, wouldn't they all get along? So the parents backed off.

What Margaret's parents didn't understand was what was going on *inside* their daughter's brain. Their daughter was obsessed with her favorite video game and was on her way to becoming addicted. Fortunately, when they saw that Margaret was not regulating herself and that family life had not improved, they sought professional help. Once her parents understood that Margaret was losing control and succumbing to an addictive process, they understood that their intervention was needed. Intervention meant setting strict and enforceable time limits on gaming, and making sure that they were engaged with their daughter, helping her find rewarding activities inside and outside the home.

If Margaret had been using pot or some other drug, her parents would have understood that it would not be wise for them to expect their daughter to regulate her drug use. We all know enough about drugs to know how dangerous they are for children. The trouble with video games (and other computer-based entertainment) is that most of us don't know they are potentially addictive. We may intuitively feel it, but we often choose not to listen to our intuition. Why? Here are some of the reasons:

As a society, we generally approve of computers. We associate them with intelligence, achievement, convenience, and "the way of the future."

We want our kids to be computer savvy so they will not be "left behind." Thus, many of us feel that whatever our kids are doing on the computer, as long as it is legal, is acceptable. We assume that if they are gaming, it is fostering, in some vaguely beneficial way, computer literacy. All around us, families are using computers. They have become an integral part of life. Our children's friends are gaming, so why not let ours, too? Our neighbors let their kids play game X, so it must be OK, right? It is this societal attitude of *acceptability* that makes it difficult for parents to take seriously their own intuitive discomfort when their children's gaming is getting out of hand.

Many of us live without extended family and are not embedded in a tight community where the intimate comings and goings of our lives are noticed. Many children are growing up feeling anonymous within their own families and communities. Fundamentally, the inattention of adults toward their children's activities allows children to get involved with on-line activities that parents might not like if they were tuned in to it. But many parents are not interested in what their children are doing with games. The fact that their children are engrossed in something that keeps them quiet is so convenient for parents that too little inquiry takes place about the content or the amount of time spent. Television has served a baby-sitting function from the 1950s to the present; computer games are now providing that service. We are not saying that parents do not love their children when they rely on technology to baby-sit them. In moderation, this need not be a problem. But, we are saying that once you, the parents, have the information we have, you may no longer feel apathetic about your children's gaming habits.

Bill

Bill's addiction was so severe that he became violent when his parents tried to take his computer away. He did not live in a happy family. His father was verbally abusive and his mother stayed away from home. The parents had never effectively set appropriate boundaries with their two children and disagreed constantly on how to parent them. When Bill found on-line gaming, he fled to that Cyber world as a refuge from the misery of his family. His parents allowed him to have a computer with Web access in his bedroom and did not seem to mind his absence from family life. By the time his parents began to notice him failing in school, Bill was deeply addicted to games, and to the on-line social life that games provide.

Bill began gaming at age twelve. Two years later, his parents tried to take his computer away. When the computer was removed, Bill began to scream and hit at his father. His anger escalated until he punched holes in his bedroom walls and generally demolished his room. Scared, his parents returned the computer to him. They did not consider calling 911 or a crisis hotline.

A year later, when Bill's grades dropped even further, his parents again removed the computer from his room. The violent scene was even worse this time. Bill ran to the kitchen, grabbed a knife, and tried to stab his father. His dad wrestled it away from him, but, once again, the parents returned the computer and never called for help. After that, the parents never again tried to take away Bill's computer out of fear that he would kill them or himself.

Children who become deeply addicted can, as this story shows, become harmful to self or others when their "drug of choice" is withdrawn. Parents are well advised to proceed with caution if their addicted child has reached such a point. In this chapter and a later one we will offer guidance about what to do if this is your situation.

Susceptibility of Children to Addiction

We do not yet know everything about biological predisposition to
addiction. (Research evidence suggests that *some* individuals may, due to
low dopamine production, be predisposed to addictions in general.)
However, there are several things we *do* know or suspect:

1. Even the healthiest children are vulnerable. The stresses of nor-
    mal life for any child are great. Learning to talk to the opposite
    sex can be hard, homework may not be enjoyable, and what
    child looks forward to doing chores? When children are allowed
    to avoid the difficult tasks of childhood and escape into video
    game play without limits, they are vulnerable to getting hooked.

2. Children with attention deficits tend to be more vulnerable.
    There are two likely reasons for this. The stimulating effect of
    video games helps children with attention deficit disorder (ADD)
    and attention deficit hyperactivity disorder (ADHD) to focus,
    just as medication would do. Also, the mental processes
    demanded by many popular video games (to scan and react in an
    ever-changing screen environment) match the mental processes
    that are strongest in many of these children.

3. Bored children who have depended on external sources of stimu-
    lation to cope with their boredom (TV viewing, for instance) are
    delighted with the external stimulation of video games. Because
    these games are interactive and tend to be more exciting than the
    passive entertainment of television, we have noticed that these
    children can quickly grow dependent on them.

4. Lonely children can easily forget about their loneliness in the
    absorbing pastime of video gaming. When these children dis-
    cover multi-user Internet gaming where they can chat with fel-

low gamers, they no longer feel so alone. In fact, many gamers feel their best friends are in their Cyber community.

5. Children with low self-esteem brought on by any number of things (poor body image, etc.) can easily find relief from their discomfort when they escape into a video game world where they can pretend to be fabulously powerful, beautiful, strong, and smart. Whatever trait or skill they believe they lack in real life is something that can easily be theirs in on-line fantasy.

6. Children living in a home where there is abuse, neglect, or other painful dynamics want to escape their emotional misery. Games offer such an escape.

7. Children with Asperger's syndrome or autism have difficulty understanding social cues and therefore find it difficult to be socially successful. Often they are bullied. Such children frequently find refuge in gaming and on-line chat, where such skills are less important.

8. Children suffering from depression or anxiety may find the world of video games a place where they can escape their unhappiness and discomfort.

Symptom Checklists and Scoring Tool

Many parents wonder if the amount of gaming in their home is appropriate or harmful. To help you decide if there is a problem, we offer the following two evaluation tools: a *self* assessment and a *parental* assessment. The self assessment can be used directly by adults and teens who are interested in evaluating themselves. The parental assessment will help adults determine whether or not a child or teen is in danger. These are tools that we have developed and found useful in our clinical work. They have not been scientifically validated. There are researchers working to develop validated tools, but in the meantime, we think you will find these helpful.

The **Signs and Symptoms of Gaming Addiction**, developed by Hilarie Cash, Ph.D. and Kim McDaniel, M.A., are shown on the following pages.

Self Assessment

Please answer the following checklist with honesty. Be aware that denial (What? Me gaming too much? I only play forty hours a week!) can influence your own judgment. If you are in doubt as to how to answer a question, ask for feedback from a trusted friend or relative — someone you know will give you a straight answer.

- ☐ Unable to predict the amount of time spent on gaming
- ☐ Failed attempts to control personal gaming behavior for an extended period of time
- ☐ Having a sense of euphoria (an exaggerated sense of well-being) while playing
- ☐ Craving more gaming
- ☐ Neglecting family and friends
- ☐ Feeling restless, irritable, and discontented when not gaming
- ☐ Lying to family or authority figures about gaming behavior
- ☐ Problems with school or job performance as a result of time spent gaming
- ☐ Having guilt, shame, anxiety, or depression as a result of time spent on gaming
- ☐ Changing sleep patterns
- ☐ Developing health issues such as carpel tunnel syndrome, eye strain, weight change, and backaches
- ☐ Denying, rationalizing, and minimizing the adverse consequences of gaming
- ☐ Withdrawing from real-life hobbies and social interactions
- ☐ Obsessing about romantic/sexual acting out through gaming
- ☐ Creating an enhanced persona to find Cyber love or Cyber sex

Evaluating Your Score

0 – 2:   Gaming is not a problem for you at this time. You know that a game is just a game. You are keeping it light and keeping it fun. The way you spend your leisure time is in balance and you're probably fine.

3 – 4:   Gaming is becoming problematic. Most likely someone close to you has expressed their concern. If you do not change your habits now, you could very easily find yourself addicted to gaming. An answer of 4 indicates abuse. It is no longer "just a game."

5 or more: Gaming has become addictive. It's time to ask for help from your friends or family. Most gamers at this level have already noticed that they are missing out on significant parts of real life: healthy relationships, graduating from school or college, or career advancement. You are on a slippery slope. As real life becomes more disappointing and difficult, your on-line world will become even more attractive. It is time for intervention.

Parental Assessment

Are you concerned about your child's gaming habits? Go through the following checklist and answer the questions honestly. The list of symptoms is the same, but we have included cues that will help you with your responses.

☐ **Unable to predict the amount of time spent on gaming**

Older children and teens should be able to give you an estimate of how much time they will spend on a game before they start.

☐ **Failed attempts to control personal gaming behavior for an extended period of time**

Frequent power struggles over gaming; not able to stop at a predetermined time.

☐ **Having a sense of euphoria (an exaggerated sense of well-being) while playing**

Ask: How do you feel when you are in the game?

☐ **Craving more gaming**

How often does he or she talk about the game or ask to play. Is it the first thing that he is drawn to upon arriving home? Is it the last thing she wants to do at the end of her day?

☐ **Neglecting family and friends**

Would he prefer to play the game instead of playing with others? Does she opt out of family events? Are friends calling less often? Are there fewer invitations for sleepovers or events?

☐ **Feeling restless, irritable, and discontented when not gaming**

Is he unhappy when he's not gaming? Is there an increase in anger and fighting when he is unplugged?

☐ **Lying to family or authority figures about gaming behavior**

There are software programs that will track the amount of time spent on gaming. Have you ever had to lock up the keyboard, disconnect the modem, or hide the mouse because you don't trust your child?

☐ **Problems with school or job performance as a result of time spent gaming**

A decline of school grades after the introduction of a new game; missing her first class of the day or often tardy at school? Are there power struggles around homework? Has he been unwilling to seek a part-time job? Has she been fired for poor attendance?

☐ **Feelings of guilt, shame, anxiety, or depression as a result of time spent on gaming**

Would your child feel proud to talk to parents or teachers about his gaming habits?

☐ **Changing sleep patterns**

Gaming all night and sleeping the day away wreaks havoc with the body's natural rhythms and establishes patterns that are difficult to reverse.

☐ **Developing health issues such as carpel tunnel syndrome, eye strain, weight change, and backaches**

Weight gain or loss of ten to fifteen pounds or more; a need to change the prescription strength for eyeglasses or contact lenses; increased difficulty with physically demanding activities.

☐ **Denying, rationalizing, and minimizing adverse consequences stemming from gaming**

"I don't have a problem," "My friends play a lot more than I do," "You're too old to understand," "I can stop any time," "It's no big deal," "I have lots of friends on-line, so it's not like I'm spending time alone."

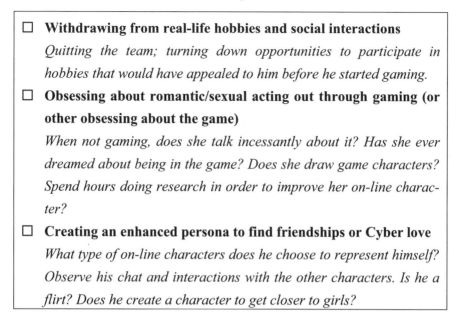

☐ **Withdrawing from real-life hobbies and social interactions**

Quitting the team; turning down opportunities to participate in hobbies that would have appealed to him before he started gaming.

☐ **Obsessing about romantic/sexual acting out through gaming (or other obsessing about the game)**

When not gaming, does she talk incessantly about it? Has she ever dreamed about being in the game? Does she draw game characters? Spend hours doing research in order to improve her on-line character?

☐ **Creating an enhanced persona to find friendships or Cyber love**

What type of on-line characters does he choose to represent himself? Observe his chat and interactions with the other characters. Is he a flirt? Does he create a character to get closer to girls?

Evaluating Your Child's Score

0 – 2:   Gaming is not a problem for your child. You encourage him to keep it light, keep it fun. You may have already established fair rules and boundaries for gaming. Stay involved. Be willing to enforce your rules and help your child maintain a healthy balance.

3 – 4:   Gaming is becoming problematic for your child. It is time to review your house rules regarding gaming and establish healthier boundaries. You may be afraid to set more stringent limits but if you do not change your child's habits now, you could very easily find him addicted to gaming. If that occurs, it will be that much more difficult to teach him how to gain control over his habit. Self-regulation is no longer an option.

5 or more: Gaming has become addictive for your child. The establishment of real-world connections has given way to video game personas. And every day that goes by increases the potential damage for children and teens. These real-world connections are essential for healthy psychosocial development. It's time to get help. Family members are noticing what the child fails to see — that he is missing out on significant parts of real life. Your child needs your help.

Multiple Addictions

Children who are addicted to video games may have multiple addictions and parents would do well to investigate that possibility. Our clinical experience and anecdotal evidence has led us to conclude that addictions most likely to *co-occur* with video game addiction involve sex, "love," and drugs.

Sex Addiction

If a child has unrestricted access to the Internet and you do not keep close tabs on what sites your child visits, it is possible for your child to discover sex sites and become addicted to them without you realizing it. The combination of children's natural curiosity about sex, their sex drive, psychological factors that can drive addictive behavior, plus the accessibility and aggressive marketing of pornography on the Internet, allow for pornography to become a regular part of many gamers' lives. The scenario that the authors hear most often is when a gamer, spending hours on the Internet and already having discovered sex sites, uses pornography for sexual release whenever he or she feels horny, bored, lonely, etc. The gamer can be involved in a game and also have a sex site open. When there is a boring period in the game, the gamer can pass the time looking at pornography and masturbating.

Many of the video game addicts that we work with have not developed their social skills, are not dating, and, in fact, are afraid to date. Yet, physically, they are in the period of their lives when sex drive is at its highest. Sexual energy is, to some degree, sublimated into the games, but, often it is dealt with in the manner we have described. If a sex addiction develops, it follows the same course as gaming addiction, and has similar signs and symptoms.

Gary

Gary offers us a good example of a gamer with dual (or co-occurring) addictions. He was referred to us by a community college counseling center when it became clear that he needed help to overcome his gaming addiction. His grades were slipping badly. When he arrived, however, we learned that he had a severe addiction to pornography in the form of Japanese *anime* (cartoons). He had spent years looking at this and other types of pornography. He had been a video game and sex addict since the age of fifteen. In high school, he had engaged in highly risky behavior, accessing porn from school computers and masturbating in the library. He was never caught masturbating, but he was caught looking at porn and was briefly suspended from school. He was filled with deep shame about his behavior, but was unable to control himself. Fortunately, there are 12-step programs for sex addicts. Through a combination of individual and group counseling, as well as 12-step work, Gary is addressing his dual addictions and regaining a sense of control over his life.

To learn more about sex addiction, we recommend reading the books by Patrick Carnes, Ph.D., especially *Out of the Shadows* and *In the Shadows of the Net*.

Love Addiction

Love addiction is a term that covers several addictive patterns having to do with romance, flirtation, fantasy, and obsession about relationships. Video gamers are often playing games that have a strong social component to them. When players of opposite genders meet and play together, romance can blossom. There are many games where this can easily happen. Recently, a couple came for counseling because the wife was deeply addicted to a game called Second Life. She already had had one "love affair" and was on her second. She had never met her "lovers," but had engaged in a mutual fantasy where, in the game, they met, chatted, "fell in love," set up a house together, and lived as husband and wife (including having Cyber sex). She was profoundly obsessed with her fantasy life, furiously denied having a problem, and yet admitted to making plans to leave her husband and two children in order to be with one of these lovers and "start a new life." This is a classic example of love addiction. She was addicted to the dopamine high she experienced as she engaged in her fantasy love affair, yet was in full denial about it. Her love and gaming addictions were so intertwined as to be indistinguishable.

In another case, parents brought to counseling their seventeen-year-old son who was deeply addicted to World of Warcraft. It soon became clear that he had an on-line romance with a female player who lived in another state. This was someone he had never met, but he was convinced of their love. He was furious with his parents for not allowing him to visit her. His obsessive behavior was a red flag that an addictive process was at work. After an intervention and time away from gaming, this young man still felt deeply attached to his fantasy romance, which he tried to continue even though he was not allowed to game. He was agitated and angry with his parents for not allowing him to return to gaming because he wanted to spend more time talking to this woman. He knew that because she spent so much time in the game, she would not have time for him if he stopped. Because he was addicted to his romantic fantasy, he found himself in excruciating withdrawal when he could not get access to her through the game.

To learn more about love addiction, we recommend Pia Mellody's *Facing Love Addiction*.

Drugs

Game addicts who are able to go without sleep have a distinct gaming advantage. Remember, many of the most highly addictive games are available for play twenty-four hours a day, seven days a week. Staying up all night while staying awake for work or school is extremely difficult, and becomes more and more taxing if tried repeatedly. Yet there are many gamers who do just this. It is no surprise, therefore, that stimulants (including highly caffeinated "power drinks") are popular with gamers. Drugs to induce sleep become necessary, too. It is a vicious cycle that can lead to drug as well as video game dependency.

There is another reason why drugs may be bundled with video game play. Gamers report that drugs like marijuana (pot) can enhance the gaming experience. Remember, an addict develops tolerance to his or her drug of choice. In the case of video games, a gamer develops tolerance to a certain amount or type of game play. What once felt thrilling or enchanting may begin to feel less stimulating. Greater stimulation is needed to get the high. Adding drugs to the mix brings a new, *double high* from the game and from the drug. In the addictive cycle, we can predict that tolerance will develop over time, as will a need for greater stimulation from some source.

Co-dependence

There is one more concept that may be helpful for parents as they try to understand why gaming addiction develops in families. Many of our readers are familiar with the term *co-dependence*. Yet unless you have done serious work around addiction, this concept may be vague to you. Even those who have studied co-dependence admit that it is a complex concept that can be hard to grasp.

Remember Rob, the sixteen-year-old who appeared earlier in this chapter? His story is one that can illustrate co-dependence. If you recall, Rob's mother was the person who first contacted us, looking for help. Rob wanted help, but his mother did not require him to make the call on his own behalf. *By doing for him what he was capable of doing for himself*, she was "care-taking" him in a co-dependent way.

This is not to imply that it is wrong to reach out and make the calls that could get help for your child. In Rob's case, the pattern of co-dependence began earlier, starting with his mother's unwillingness to set firm limits on his gaming. She had given up trying to control his behavior because nothing she tried had worked. She gradually increased her tolerance of his behavior until she began accepting something she once would have thought impossible to accept. She allowed him to live at home, remain unemployed, and flunk out of high school. She felt angry, worried, and helpless. She wanted to be part of his *solution*, but in fact became part of his *problem*.

The language of co-dependence sounds reasonable, but on closer scrutiny, you can begin to hear the excuses being made that keep an addiction going. We understand that parents' intentions are good and that co-dependent parents are typically kind, confused, and seekers of harmony. But for kids in trouble, these good intentions, without adequate action and limits, are actually damaging. Here are some of the co-dependent statements we typically hear:

"At least he is home."
"I don't worry about him driving drunk."
"I just want him to be happy."
"I want peace and quiet."
"I am too busy at work."

When there are serious problems in a family (alcoholism; anger; hostility between parents; mental illness; physical, verbal, or sexual abuse), parents are even more likely to find reasons and excuses to not set effective limits with a child's problematic game play. This, too, is a type of co-dependence. Until at least one parent faces up to the seriousness of the dysfunction within the family and takes constructive action to address it (such as seeking professional help), the child's problem with video gaming will not be dealt with effectively.

Bill, whom we also met earlier, was such a child. His parents were in a miserable marriage. They fought constantly. The father was addicted to alcohol and pornography; the mother was a co-dependent who escaped life by staying away from home as much as possible. She knew that Bill was in trouble with his on-line gaming, but she was in too much denial about her whole situation to take effective action. His father knew Bill was in trouble, but was so steeped in his own addiction that he was unable to be effective in dealing with his son. He refused to assume the responsibility of good parenting.

When parents are in a co-dependent relationship with their child, it is as if they are acting as *co-conspirators* in keeping the addictive habit alive. In other words, the parent receives a benefit or "payoff" from their child's behavior. We know this sounds harsh. And we know that parents usually are not doing this consciously. But denial is a powerful force. We would like to shake you out of your denial if you are in it, so that you can take more effective action.

Alex

To illustrate this, let's look at the case of Alex. Alex was a fourteen-year-old boy who had been gaming extensively since he was very young. He started with hand-held devices, graduated to console games, and then discovered the Internet. His mom was single and worked long hours, including many weekends. With her gone so much, Alex found himself alone or home with his brother after school. There was a period of years when they moved frequently and often lived in rough neighborhoods. Mom did not have much discretionary income, but she managed to keep her children supplied with the latest gaming technology. From her perspective, the computers kept her boys entertained and at home when she couldn't be there. She felt pride in their expertise and embraced the notion that she was giving her kids a "leg up" in life. When Alex's grades began to drop in middle school, his mother tried to limit the time he spent gaming. She found this hard to enforce, however. For years they engaged in an unproductive cycle of mom's anger and lectures, followed by imposed limitations that were soon forgotten. Alex argued back in the heat of the moment, but knew that all he had to do was wait and he would soon be able to get back to gaming as usual.

What Alex's mom failed to do was get rid of the games and take control of the computer. Why? Fear and guilt replaced her pride and her sense of doing the best for her child. She feared what would happen if she stopped his gaming: he might go out into the world and get in trouble with sex and drugs; he might stop loving her. She felt guilty for being such an absent parent and wanted to make up for it by giving her son access to the thing he seemed to want most. And, she did not want to give up what made life comfortable for them both. If Alex no longer had the thing that took his full attention, he would be much more "in her hair." She could not retreat at the end of a long and exhausting day into the privacy of her bedroom to watch TV and relax. This is co-dependence at work.

Identifying and overcoming co-dependence is difficult for anyone, especially parents. If your child's gaming behavior has become problematic, perhaps even addictive, it is important to ask yourself this question:

"What's in it for me?" When you can answer this, you will be able to see the role you have played in the development of the problem and recognize that you must *change yourself* to set things right.

Conclusion

An addiction is hard to shake at any age. Look at the time, money, and repeated effort that many alcoholics go through when they try to recover. We know that the younger a person is when he or she becomes alcoholic, the harder it is for them to live free of alcohol. If they begin drinking as children, their personalities are not fully formed. They have not learned healthy ways to cope with psychological pain and external stress. When they stop drinking, they have a tremendous amount of catching up to do.

Imagine yourself as a five-year-old becoming addicted to a dopamine high brought on by playing your favorite hand-held or console games. How likely would you be to think that something is wrong and you should stop before it gets worse? You wouldn't, of course. This is why your children need a parent to understand what is going on and intervene, setting limits that they cannot set for themselves.

If you follow our recommendations, your children will be very unhappy with you at first. They will not understand why it is in their best interests to limit something they enjoy so much. They may actually be addicted, in which case they will go through real withdrawal. In younger children this will mean tantrums, manipulations to get you to remove the limits, crankiness, tiredness, restlessness, and depression. What we want you to understand is that all of these symptoms of withdrawal will disappear with time (a few days or weeks), but only if you do not waiver in your resolve. Do not relent!

If you have a teenager with years of addiction behind him, withdrawal can be severe, even dangerous at times. Unfortunately, inpatient treatment programs for gaming addicts are a rarity. Get help and plan carefully before you proceed. Later chapters discuss more intervention options. Our main point is to help you understand that it is up to you to change the situation and to not turn aside once you have committed to a sensible course of action. You may be afraid and full of self-doubt. This is normal. But do not give in to your impulse to surrender. Your children are depending on you to be strong enough to give them the help they need.

At the same time, we want you to be cautious. If you suspect that your child may have a disorder like Asperger's syndrome, be sure to seek advice from a specialist before taking the games away. The next chapter discusses some of the disorders that can easily *co-occur* with gaming addiction. If you think your child may be suicidal or potentially violent, seek professional help before taking action!

2
Effects of Gaming
on the Body and Brain

There are three seemingly unrelated things occurring in our country that are frequently reported in the news: 1) an epidemic of attention deficit disorder (ADD) among our children; 2) an epidemic of childhood obesity (and type 2 diabetes); and 3) children spending a lot of time in front of electronic screens (computer and television). The authors are not alone in seeing the interrelatedness of these three facts. We believe that as children spend more and more time in the sedentary pursuit of playing video games and watching TV, two significant things are happening:

First, they are gaining weight at an unprecedented rate. In fact, our offspring have become the most overweight population of children in human history. Type 2 diabetes, resulting from poor eating habits, has had to be renamed. It was once called *adult-onset* diabetes. That name no longer is appropriate, with so many kids developing it.

Second, the brains of children who spend a lot of time playing video games are profoundly affected. As their brains become wired to be good at playing video games, we believe this wiring is starting to mimic ADD.

This chapter will explore the impact of video games on health and brain function. As you read, keep in mind that we are talking primarily about *excessive* gaming. The guidelines we propose here are designed to keep a child's video gaming within boundaries that will keep her or him developing in a healthy way. However, any exposure to gaming will have an impact, and you must decide the level you are comfortable with.

Keep in mind that our recommendations are based on evidence that continues to accumulate. We anticipate that further research will finally convince those who would disagree with the conclusions we have reached. It took decades of research to finally prove that marijuana is addictive, yet many people refuse to accept that conclusion. It is possible that the same thing will happen with video gaming.

The Toxic Triad

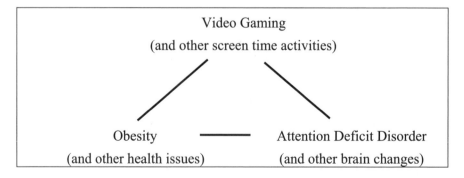

Health Hazards

It is currently estimated that nine million American children are obese or close to it. For the first time in a century, our children are expected to have, on average, a shorter life span than their parents. Physical inactivity is a primary reason. It is now clear that screen time is correlated with health problems stemming from obesity and lack of physical exercise. Obesity brings with it a whole host of problems: type 2 diabetes, high cholesterol, poor cardiovascular development, stressed joints, weakened bones (from lack of activity), and psychological problems such as low self-esteem, depression, and social anxiety. Inactivity, more generally, leads to a raft of problems in addition to those caused by obesity. Plenty of physical activity is vital to good sleep, the working off of excess energy, and the development of coordination. These benefits, in turn, lead to subtle, but important brain developments that affect a child's ability to learn, analyze, plan, and stay focused. More on this later.

Television is recognized as a culprit in this story. What has not yet been widely recognized is the role of computers. In our estimation, computers are far more problematic than simple television viewing because they *hook* the participant more completely. The dopamine high that children (and adults) experience as they game (or chat, or whatever) keeps them *stuck* to the screen. This *stickiness factor* is used by the game industry to judge the success of their games. Television shows, which probably do not elicit as much dopamine activity in the brain, have a beginning and an end. Parents can, and do, often limit TV time, or insist that their children go to bed after a particular show is finished. There are no such endings to on-line games and on-line chatting. Ending a session on-line requires either self-discipline (which children usually lack) or parental intervention.

Vision

Obesity is not the only health risk arising from unlimited gaming. Jane Healy, author of *Failure to Connect: How Computers Affect Our Children's Minds — and What We Can Do About It (1999)*, interviewed ophthalmologists who have long noted an increase in eye strain and vision problems as a result of increasing amounts of time spent in front of computer screens. Reading print on paper can strain your eyes; computers even more so, depending on a number of factors, such as amount of time, whether or not breaks are taken, and the distance of a player from the screen. This apparently has to do, among other things, with the flicker of the screen (known as the "refresh rate"), the way light reflects off of screens, the angle at which we look at screens, and the fixedness with which we stare at screens.

Some developmental optometrists believe that children spending too much time in front of screens and too little time in physical activity are not integrating their visual systems with body movement, which, in turn, has a negative impact both on perceptual/motor and mental/learning processes.

The American Optometric Association (AOA) has identified what they call Computer Vision Syndrome (CVS). It is "the complex of eye and vision problems related to near work which are experienced during or related to computer use." Symptoms most often include eyestrain, headaches, blurred distance or near vision, dry or red eyes, double vision, neck aches, backaches, and increased sensitivity to light.

There is some good news about vision and video gaming, too. There is evidence that video gaming in moderation can improve vision, eye movement skills, eye-hand coordination, visual reaction time, and peripheral awareness.

We encourage you to proceed with caution. Limit your children's screen time and make them take frequent breaks (five minutes every half hour). Make sure the lighting is not causing glare on the screen, and, if possible, arrange the screen so that your child is looking slightly down at it, not up or straight ahead. Refresh rates are not an issue if your child is using a flat screen. But if the screen is not flat, make sure the refresh rate is set at 75. And, discuss these issues with your pediatrician.

Muscular/Skeletal

Backs, wrists, and thumbs are suffering under the strain as well. Poor posture developed in childhood while playing games and from lack of exercise can lead to problems in adolescence and adulthood. Slipped discs and pinched nerves can make life miserable, and the likelihood of developing these problems increases with bad posture. Carpel tunnel syndrome and repetitive motion strain of the thumbs are showing up in gamers. The American Physical Therapy Association (APTA) has created guidelines for parents, hoping families can avoid the pain and long-term ill-effects of "Video Gamer's Thumb," which involves the tendons, nerves, and ligaments in children's hands, wrists, thumbs, and forearms. Symptoms range from fatigue and loss of strength to aches and pains, burning, and tingling. Helpful guidelines can be found at www.apta.org/consumer.

These painful conditions can perhaps be avoided if children are allowed to game only for strictly limited amounts of time, are taught good posture, kept physically active, and provided ergonomically correct furniture to use.

Sleep

Sleep deprivation is a huge problem among heavy gamers. This subject is dealt with at length in subsequent chapters on development, but we mention it here because it is so important. It is not possible for children (including adolescents) to achieve optimal development without adequate sleep. We now know that the brain is undergoing enormous changes during adolescence. Teenagers need up to 9.5 hours of nightly sleep if they are to enjoy optimal development. Video gamers are notorious for continuing with a game while ignoring their bodies' desperate need for sleep.

The authors had a client who was referred after spending a week in a psychiatric ward. He was a college student who spent his Thanksgiving break on a gaming binge. After thirty-six hours of non-stop gaming, he became psychotic (a normal response to prolonged sleep deprivation) and had to be hospitalized.

You may have read media reports about gamers in other countries who died after playing non-stop for thirty-six hours or more. Their bodies shut down, similar to the experimental rats who kept a steady drip of cocaine going directly into their brains, never stopping to eat or sleep until they died.

Coordination

Coordination, balance, and depth perception — each is a brain function that can be adversely affected by unlimited and untimely gaming. Children need to fully use their bodies to explore the physical world, running, tumbling, climbing, going in, coming out, pushing, sliding, and all the other things that normal children have done throughout human history. These activities aid the development of coordination, balance, and good depth perception and come to all children naturally. Yet the mesmerizing effect of screens can put to sleep this natural inclination toward activity. Please take heed. If you want to raise healthy children, do not allow them to become inactive.

We are interested by a news report concerning a Scandinavian country that requires military service for all adult men upon graduation from high school. Recently, the military has sent many of the new recruits home because they were unfit for duty. They were too psychologically immature and physically out of shape to handle the demands of military life; this was attributed directly to excessive video game play. It is ironic that video gaming may be fostering skills, attitudes, and perspectives in young men that precondition them to be more easily trained as efficient killers while, at the same time, rendering them physically unfit for service.

Electromagnetic Fields

There are two more physical health concerns that are controversial, but worthy of note. The first has to do with the potential health hazards of computer radiation and heat. The media has reported concerns from the medical community that laptops, resting on the laps of males, may contribute to infertility. There is evidence that as little as one hour of sitting with a laptop on the lap will raise the temperature of the testicles as much as five degrees, well above the temperature needed for good sperm production. It is not yet known if the lowering of fertility due to laptop use is long-term, or if it is due to heat or radiation, or some combination of the two.

We agree with aforementioned author Jane Healy who advises caution. "Until we know the truth, it would seem prudent to monitor children's exposure, since it is thought that children are five to ten times more vulnerable to radiation than adults. Organs and systems perhaps at risk are bone, central nervous system, and thyroid gland. Because of their small body weight, children may receive a higher amount of radiation per

pound of body weight than adults from the same amount of radiation."
She recommends that:

o   Computer users maintain a distance from the screen of thirty to
    thirty-six inches and four feet or more from the backs and sides
    of video display terminals.

o   Multiple computers, both at home or at school, should be no
    closer than four feet from one another and should never be
    placed back-to-back.

o   Children should never study or sleep directly behind a computer
    on the other side of a wall as magnetic fields can penetrate walls.

o   Only computers with low electromagnetic field (EMF) radiation
    should be considered for purchase.

o   Computers should be turned off or put in sleep mode when not in
    use.

We hope that parents teach their children to use laptops from a
tabletop, not a lap.

Seizures

Our second *electromagnetic* concern has to do with the increase in video
game-related epileptic seizures that, although rare, do occur in some
children who have no prior history of epilepsy. Video game epilepsy is a
variant of photosensitive reflex epilepsy. The epilepsy *trigger area* in the
brains of photosensitive individuals is connected to the visual processing
area of the brain and is sensitive to a *trigger stimulus*, a light display
outside of the body (strobe lights, for instance) that flashes between ten
and thirty times per second.

When the trigger stimulus is witnessed by the photosensitive individual, the trigger area begins firing abnormally. This abnormal firing
spreads to other areas of the brain. In sensitive individuals, video games

may provoke a seizure with symptoms ranging from nausea, listlessness, and headaches to short seizures (in which the child stares for a few moments and then, with a start, returns to normal) to full-blown seizures (stiffening, shaking, brief loss of consciousness). If you see any of these signs in your child, cease all video gaming and see a pediatrician immediately.

Mental Health Risks and Co-occurring Disorders

There are a number of psychiatric disorders that may co-occur with video game addiction. Many symptoms may be the *result* of video game addiction. It is our belief that prolonged, addictive video game play can influence the brain to such an extent that it may, in effect, cause signs and symptoms of these disorders. We hope that as you read, you will gain some idea of what behaviors in your child may indicate a problem worthy of professional consultation and intervention.

We have provided information here that may help you decide if your child needs a mental health evaluation by a professional. There are many reputable sites on the Internet, such as www.mayoclinic.com, that contain valuable information about the following disorders. We recommend you read up on any disorders described briefly here or any others that may concern your child.

Normal Anxiety and Anxiety Disorders

Everyone experiences anxiety and fear, which are appropriate responses to environmental threats. Some of us are more prone to be anxious than others. Children who are naturally anxious are often perceived as shy, timid, or cautious. There is nothing wrong with this and, as the old saying goes, "It takes all kinds to make a world."

If you have such a child, you should be alert, however, to the allure of video games and the Internet, where such a child can escape the often-frightening challenges in the real world. Hiding behind a screen feels safe for kids who are anxious, whether their anxiety is normal or not. Allowing them to hide there, spending hours in front of the screen, is often the very opposite of what such children need. If you have a naturally anxious child, he or she needs practice in the real world to build skills that will increase confidence and reduce anxiety.

Typical signs of anxiety would include edginess, restlessness, difficulty concentrating, irritability, timidity, difficulty with sleep, and physical symptoms like muscle tension, headache, stomach complaints, and diarrhea.

Social anxiety is a subtype of a generalized anxiety disorder and, as the name implies, is primarily related to social situations. Typical signs and symptoms include intense fear and avoidance of social situations (especially with strangers), excessive worry about embarrassment or humiliation, fear of being judged, difficulty making eye contact, and physical symptoms like sweating, flushing, shaky voice, heart palpitations, and clammy hands.

Many video game addicts show signs and symptoms of social anxiety when they interact with people in the real world, especially with those they do not know or know well. You, the parent, might notice that these kids seem to be having a wonderfully sociable time when they are playing games (whether at a LAN party with their gamer friends or over the Internet) but poorly handle their face-to-face interactions outside of gaming. You might be tempted to think that the gaming is a constructive way to fill the social void, but caution is advised. There is evidence that gaming can contribute to the development of social anxiety. As always, it is the amount of time spent at the computer versus time spent in the real world that makes the difference. Moderate gaming may be of social benefit to your child; too much time may be harmful. Hard and unpleasant as it may be for your anxious child, we believe that plenty of real-world social experience is needed to build the social skills he or she needs to feel confident. If you have a socially anxious child, extra help from you may be required to create real-world experiences that will be of benefit.

Asperger's Syndrome

Our experience has been that youth who have Asperger's syndrome are strongly drawn to the world of the Internet and video gaming. This is because they feel safe behind a screen where they are not face-to-face, yet they can enjoy social interaction and entertainment. We have also noticed that a child who does not have true Asperger's syndrome, yet has been gaming for years in an addictive way, can develop symptoms that mimic Asperger's (social avoidance, poor social skills, and obsession with gaming).

The following was contributed by our colleague Elaine Duncan, a therapist who specializes, among other things, in autism spectrum disorders and video game addiction:

If your child has an autism spectrum disorder, he or she may be at greater risk than the general population to become addicted to computer gaming. He probably finds the social world to be a frightening place and prefers to spend his free time playing computer games. What begins as a safe, stress-reducing activity can become his social life, and often his entire life.

What is an autism spectrum disorder? The effects of autism show up in a continuum, or spectrum, of severity. All autism disorders are developmental disorders. In other words, they appear very early in life. Usually by age three or earlier, parents know that their child is not developing in quite the expected way. Their offspring probably had difficulty forming peer relationships, or perhaps didn't show any interest in having friends. As they became teens and young adults, they may have wanted to have friends, but didn't understand the rules of social interaction and therefore found making friends difficult. Communication skills probably did not develop at the expected rate, and the ability to carry on a conversation was highly impaired. The rate and quality of speech may have been abnormal and the content may have been restricted to the child's particular, intense interest.

On the high end of the spectrum, "high-functioning autism" or Asperger's syndrome is difficult to diagnosis early in life. Those children may have received an array of diagnoses such as attention deficit hyperactivity disorder (ADHD), depression, anxiety disorders, and obsessive-compulsive disorder (OCD). But many parents often discover that these diagnoses don't really fit. They feel in their hearts that there is something that would better describe their child. To make things even more confusing, ADHD, depression, anxiety, and OCD may co-occur with Asperger's syndrome.

Teens and young adults with Asperger's syndrome (or Asperger's disorder) usually have average to above-average intelligence, but have great difficulty with social interactions. By this age, they have had a lot of failures in attempts to make friends, and often retreat to the safety of their computer. For an "Aspie," computers make a lot more sense than people because they're logical and predictable. In addition, people are noisy and people with Asperger's are usually highly sensitive to sound, touch, smells, and lights. So, interacting with the computer in the bedroom is appealing. These folks are very susceptible to making their friends on the Internet, friends whom they may never meet but fulfill their fantasy of having a social life.

Misunderstanding and inappropriate use of nonverbal behaviors are hallmarks of Asperger's syndrome. Someone with Asperger's will usually make very little, if any, eye contact. He or she will have difficulty understanding subtle clues (for instance, when a person is bored by the topic of conversation), appropriate behavior in social settings (how loud to speak or when to enter a conversation), and how to know if someone of the opposite sex is interested. He will have difficulty making friendships with peers and may have more friends who are significantly older or younger. Problems making friends have probably caused him a lot of pain and, by adolescence, he may well be experiencing depression. Indeed, a lifetime of failure and social rejections may have plunged him into a deep, suicidal depression.

Individuals on the spectrum also struggle with anxiety that is often related to their difficulty with the social world. Therefore, they frequently isolate to soothe themselves, even though, at heart, they want to fit in and have friends. They will seek ways to soothe or escape from their anxiety, such as playing computer games. Stress is such a problem for individuals on the spectrum that they are much more likely to spend inordinate hours on their computers, just to calm their jangled nerves. Therefore, if it becomes necessary to greatly restrict their computer use, parents are advised to plan for a replacement stress-reducer.

If you suspect your child has an autism spectrum disorder, a neuropsychologist or clinical psychologist specializing in the disorder should be able to make a diagnosis for you. Autism is

*becoming more prevalent (for reasons as yet unknown), and
practitioners who are not specialists may still be familiar enough
with the disorder to recognize it. Early diagnosis is important
because there are a number of interventions that can help. Even if
your child is an adult, he or she will be much better off getting a
proper diagnosis and seeking treatment. Although there is currently
no cure for autism, there are several types of therapies that can help
mitigate autism's effects and help an individual lead a satisfying life.*

Depression

Our experience has been that depressed children seek escape from their
feelings, and video gaming offers a very convenient and engrossing
escape. However, video game addiction, like all addictions, can also
produce depression.

Research has revealed a strong correlation between depression and
the amount of time spent on-line. For a child who is an addict, chasing a
dopamine high in spite of negative consequences (school failure, social
isolation, and sleep deprivation) can easily lead to depression. It is not
easy for a parent to determine which came first. If you take an honest
look at what is happening inside the family (marital conflict or divorce,
etc.), the chronic or unusual stressors your child is dealing with (major
relocation, etc.), and the history of depression and addiction on both
sides of the family, you may be able to make a good guess as to whether
or not your child's depression is largely an outcome of video gaming.
Whatever your conclusion, if you see signs of depression, it's a good
idea to seek professional advice.

The most common symptoms of depression are depressed mood
(crying, sadness, hopelessness, helplessness), social withdrawal, and loss
of interest in normal, daily activities. In addition, you may notice other

signs and symptoms such as difficulty with sleep, reduced concentration, fatigue, agitation, anxiety, and changes in weight.

ADD (Attention Deficit Disorder) and ADHD (Attention Deficit Hyperactivity Disorder)

Teachers are complaining more and more about the increasing numbers of children who have trouble maintaining proper attention in their classrooms. The more extreme of these children may end up with a diagnosis of ADD or ADHD even when there is no family history of this disorder.

Research has demonstrated that ADD has a strong genetic basis. If this is true, then why are so many cases of ADD being diagnosed and treated with medication? There is good reason to believe it is tied to children's heavy involvement with TV and video gaming. As we discuss elsewhere in the chapter, we believe that because video gaming is *interactive*, its effects on the brain are more powerful than TV. Research is beginning to suggest that one of the effects seen with the popular *quick scan and react* battle games, is that the brain development they promote mimics ADD. To stay alive in the game, the player must constantly survey dangerous territory and react quickly, shooting before being shot.

Children with ADD tend to be highly attracted to these types of games, probably because their brains are already wired to handle them well. And because the games help them stay focused, they produce an effect similar to that of Ritalin, a stimulant. Our concern is that children without ADD could end up with something akin to ADD simply by playing these video games to the exclusion of balanced development. They could have trouble maintaining normal focus and attention in the classroom and in other areas of their lives.

Children with ADD tend to be highly distractible, do not tend to pay close attention to details, make careless mistakes, have difficulty with follow-through and organization, tend to be forgetful, and, often, do not listen well. Children who are also hyperactive may fidget and squirm, run and climb excessively, talk excessively, often interrupt, and have difficulty playing quietly. There are many good books that discuss ADD and we urge parents to educate yourselves if you think your child has it.

There are other mental health diagnoses that we have not discussed here. The ones covered are the ones, in our experience, most likely to show up. Always be alert and attuned to your child, and if you have questions and concerns, do not hesitate to seek professional advice.

Will Video Games Make My Kid Smarter?

Recent research using technology that takes images of the brain at work demonstrates that *far more of the brain is involved in the simple task of adding numbers than in playing a popular video game.* During video game play, only a relatively small section of the brain is active, whereas almost the whole brain is involved in the arithmetic task. Are you surprised? Many people are because it is widely assumed that video gaming makes children smarter.

Video game play powerfully affects the way a child's brain develops. Is this a good or a bad thing? Does it make my child smarter or not? Am I preparing my child for the future? How much is too much? Naturally, parents care about the answers to these questions. For an in-depth discussion of these questions and the answers that research is providing, we again encourage you to read Jane Healy's excellent book, *Failure to Connect: How Computers Affect Our Children's Minds—and What We Can Do About It (1999)*. She writes:

Human brains arrive in the world with excess potential to make connections (synapses) between different types of neurons. As a youngster carries out certain types of activities, those connections are strengthened, whereas habits that don't get much stimulation or practice may lack a strong neural base. Repetition of an experience tends to "set" connections to make that particular form of learning more automatic. Many children with school problems lack strong automatic connections for particular academic skills, such as reading or math computation, or for learning habits such as attention, strategic problem-solving, or self-control. The difficulty may be exacerbated because somewhere along the line their brain didn't get the proper experience to set up a strong basis for those particular abilities. Age-appropriate computer use may help establish some forms of connections, but inappropriate use may also build resistant habits that interfere with academic learning. Once set into the brain's connectivity, such patterns are hard to break.

Brains tend to become custom-tailored for skills that the environment promotes. For most of us who spent many childhood years practicing language and reading, for example, many brain connections have become specialized for these media. If we had grown up in a totally screen-based culture, with icons instead of written text, our reading connections might have withered away in favor of strong visual systems. In fact, we are already seeing a new emphasis on "visual intelligence" supplementing verbal forms.

What kinds of connections will our children need most? I advocate giving them the widest repertoire possible so they will be equipped to deal with multiple eventualities. A child with lopsided experiences is likely to end up with a lopsided brain.

When parents and teachers reflect on this information, they begin to think seriously about what mental aptitudes are really most important to promote. I have asked a lot of folks in workshops to come up with a list of their choices of "skills for the future." The things they tend to focus on are not technical skills; rather they nominate mental habits like analytic thinking and problem-solving, communication abilities, imagination, values, persistence, creativity, kindness, and tolerance.

The development of each and every one of these listed skills has the potential to be negatively affected by overuse and untimely introduction of video games and computers. Based on our search of the literature and our clinical experience, we recommend, for developmentally normal children, waiting until they are seven years of age before introducing them to any computer technology. Making sure they have age-appropriate toys and plenty of loving interaction with caregivers helps ensure development of their full potential.

After age seven, we recommend only limited and carefully chosen software for children. If appropriate care is not taken and lopsided development occurs in the brain, the following problems are more likely to occur:

o   Shortened attention span
o   Reduced critical thinking
o   Reduced creativity and imagination
o   Reduced ability to be internally motivated and self-directed
o   Lowered frustration tolerance
o   Cognitive desensitization (aggression)
o   Limited language development

o   Visual deficits (depth perception, near-sightedness, computer-vision syndrome)

Healy continues:

In addition to altering society, new technologies also have a disconcerting habit of changing the mental skills and even the brain organization of people using them. Historically, one of the most profound examples of this neurological reorganization accompanied the advent of language, which furthered the size and power of the left-hemisphere systems for logical, analytical thought. More recently, scientists have observed that even differences between pictorial languages (Japanese writing, for example) and alphabetic scripts of European languages cause physical alterations during brain development. Fast-paced, nonlinguistic, and visually distracting television may literally have changed children's minds, making sustained attention to verbal input, such as reading or listening, far less appealing than faster-paced visual stimuli.

Debate rages among parents and educators as to whether and how computers should be used with young children. Thus far, however, public discussion of technology has skirted important questions of age-appropriate use, with marketers cheering when someone opines: "The earlier the better. Let's prepare these kids for the future." Yet, as we have seen, preparation for the future involves a far different set of abilities. Time spent with computers in the early years not only subtracts from important developmental tasks but may also entrench bad learning habits, leading to poor motivation and even symptoms of learning disability.

Academic Skills

Critical and analytical thinking are related skills that require a person to think logically about a subject and ask critical questions. The thinker aims to understand the concepts involved and logical weaknesses in the presented arguments. These mental processes require inward-focused, sustained attention, which is hard to develop in an environment of constant, external distraction. Quiet, peaceful time is ideal for promoting these and other abilities, such as creativity and imagination.

James Paul Gee, in his book, *What Video Games Have to Teach Us about Learning and Literacy*, argues that the best video games promote certain types of analytical thinking. This is likely true, but a problem arises when *life* experience is limited by *gaming* experience. It takes time and motivation to figure out how to be successful in a social situation, or how to give a teacher what she wants in a term paper. Such thinking and learning will promote analytical thinking and will help a child succeed in the real world that he or she must inhabit. Figuring out how to kill aliens may promote analytical thinking, but, having little real-world relevance, may fail to transfer to real-world situations. Some video games are designed to be relevant to the real world, and we encourage you, the parents, to find those you think will be the most meaningful and relevant.

Most parents realize that creativity and a vivid imagination are valuable assets for their children. What parents may not realize is the inverse correlation between screen time and these mental processes. When a child spends a lot of time in front of a screen, visual images are being provided to that child — images that came out of someone else's imagination. And when a child plays a game, the rules of that game were created by someone else's imagination. *The child is not the author of his or her own imaginatively created games*, and is not generating his or her own fanciful images to accompany that game. Free, imaginative play and reading (or being read to) are activities that promote a child's creativity and imagination. Too much screen time can put a damper on their development.

Related to this is the development of internal motivation and self-direction. We are finding that children who are heavily dependent on video gaming (and other screen-time activities) for their entertainment are showing deficits in their ability to set goals for themselves and follow through to achieve them. They appear to lack motivation, which may, in turn, be related to a reduced ability to think creatively, analytically, and imaginatively. Their lack of motivation may also be related to lack of resourcefulness. When children do not spend their time finding practical solutions to real-world problems, they may lack the skills and self-confidence that would make them resourceful. Finally, when children depend on immediate gratification for their motivation, they have trouble doing many normal things in the real world if these things are not *immediately* rewarding.

Frustration tolerance is the ability to delay gratification, to wait, to be patient, to handle the emotion of frustration without a "melt-down." Professionals in education and the mental health fields are noting that the children of today who are heavily dependent on screen time are less and less able to delay gratification and properly handle their frustrations. Video games themselves tend to be all-consuming of a player's attention. The rewards are *intermittent*, meaning that they are unpredictable but frequent enough to keep the player trying. Once engrossed in a video game, the rewards of playing come frequently enough to hook the player. Think, by comparison, of the skills a child must develop to sustain activities that are not so immediately rewarding.

Consider the building of a fort or baking cookies. Slow, careful steps must be followed or figured out if the goal is to be achieved. If a child is learning these skills for the first time, much frustration will be experienced as mistakes are made or as skills are figured out and practiced. Rewards may come along the way, or perhaps at the end. Children of all ages with low frustration tolerance tend to give up easily rather than persist patiently until the task is accomplished and the reward experienced.

We must emphasize to parents the value of children persisting in the pursuit of a goal, which means doggedly trying to attain it in spite of frustration. In a longitudinal study by the late psychologist John Digman, the personality factor that most predicted success in adulthood was *persistence*. Parents may have the mistaken idea that their children are showing persistence when they see them playing a game for many hours. To the contrary, their children are feeling highly rewarded by the activity of gaming, so there may actually be very little persistence required. Persistence involves *delaying* gratification; gaming involves experiencing the intervals of gratification that are just right to keep the player playing. Children who have become addicted to gaming will pursue their euphoria, even as it becomes harder and harder to achieve, as it does in many games. That is not the persistence we are talking about. We are talking, for example, about a child grinding their way through difficult homework because they want to get a good grade. The reward may not come until weeks or months later, although a healthy child will gain some satisfaction from facing and overcoming the academic challenges involved in that day's homework.

Jane Healy writes:

> *In one study, preschoolers' self control was assessed by determining whether they could delay the instant gratification of eating one marshmallow in favor of waiting fifteen to twenty minutes for the promise of two marshmallows. Fourteen years later, the same*

children were evaluated; those who had been able to control their behavior were more emotionally stable, better liked by teachers and peers, and scored an average of 210 points higher on the SAT. While such correlation studies do not prove that this one ability [self-control] caused the differences, factors far beyond IQ are increasingly associated with effective mental habits.

Tom is a twenty-four-year-old gamer who talks about his struggle to persist in tasks that are not immediately rewarding. He has recently returned to college after flunking out. He spent six years gaming to the exclusion of almost everything else. He describes self-discipline as being like a muscle that has atrophied. It has been a profound struggle for him to build up this muscle or *habit of mind* in order to succeed in college. He practices by doing Sudoku puzzles and memorizing Japanese. Self-discipline is still a struggle for him, and may be for the rest of his life. Only time will tell.

Love and the Development of Conscience

The brain is not an organ for intellectual work only. It is also the organ whose wiring will determine moral beliefs, emotional experience, and social skills. Later chapters will examine these developmental imperatives in detail. In this chapter, we will provide an overview of how inappropriate and untimely video gaming may negatively affect the brain development required for love and the development of morality and conscience. As time advances and more research is brought to bear on this subject, we will be able to speak with greater authority on this matter. The research so far is justifying our worry, but the phenomenon of video gaming on a mass level is so new that research is scrambling to catch up.

Martha Stout, in her excellent book, *The Sociopath Next Door*, discusses the way in which conscience develops. Her primary point, based on a careful review of the available research, is that our conscience grows naturally out of our love, caring, and attachment to others. If we care about someone, then we feel guilty if we behave in a way that is harmful or hurtful to them. Sociopaths, however, are incapable of true attachment, and therefore incapable of conscience. Their problem appears to be genetically predisposed, but the expression of sociopathic behavior can be greatly influenced by the culture into which a sociopath is born. When the cultural norm places the welfare of the social group above the individual, the sociopath is more likely to conform to cultural expectations and, therefore, refrain from expressing his or her individual self-interest and behave within normal bounds. When the cultural norm emphasizes individual self-interest above that of the group, the setting is ripe for the sociopath to get away with pursuing self-interest, employing any behavior that gets him what he wants. These behaviors might be bullying, manipulating, lying, etc. If they are perfected by adulthood, they are likely to remain unchecked unless the sociopath is caught by the legal system.

Stout argues that present-day American culture is *an individualistic culture where sociopathic behavior is able to flourish* and such behavior is found in about four percent of the population.

What about the development of conscience in the other 96 percent? How well does our culture support the development of strong ties of attachment and love, the foundation of conscience, in those who have no predisposition toward sociopathy?

A related question is: how well do we, as a culture, teach right and wrong behavior? We can love someone and have a guilty conscience if we know we have harmed them, but what about those with whom we have no personal relationship?

If Stout is right, then 96 percent of the population wants to feel strong bonds of attachment, to love and be loved. And they want to be taught correct behavior, behavior that will allow them to fit in with the cultural norm and avoid the pricks of a guilty conscience. Increasingly, these two needs are not being well met by our culture. There are a number of reasons for this, and screen time is one of them.

All children need to feel securely nestled in their families. When this security is absent, a child feels a desperate longing for the attachments that are missing. For a person feeling a lack of emotional security, safety, and love, screen time provides a distraction and a substitute. *On-line communities substitute for real-life communities.* Stimulating/medicating video games dull the pain of what is missing from real life.

A valid question is: So what? What is wrong with this substitution? Isn't it just as good? The answer, we believe, is "no." Video gaming and the Internet do a poor job of developing the attachments we need in order to develop a conscience and a moral compass.

As will be discussed later in the chapters on child development, no child can grow and thrive, physically and emotionally, without secure attachments to his or her caregivers. Humans are not self-regulating organisms. We thrive only through our relationships. If we are deprived of these attachments, we suffer and, if we are infants, we may die. Ample evidence from orphanages around the world attest to the horrors that happen to children whose most basic attachment needs are not met. They do not thrive; many die in infancy.

On the other hand, normal children who attach to caregivers who are well attuned and responsive to that child's needs are likely to develop well.

Lewis, Amini, and Lannon, in *A General Theory of Love*, wrote:

A baby begins life as an open loop. His mother's milk provides nourishment, and her limbic (emotional) communication provides synchronization for his delicate neural rhythms. As a child matures, his neurophysiology internalizes some regulatory functions. Balanced from the outside in, his brain learns stability.

Lengthy parental absence deprives a child of limbic regulation. If he is very young, losing his parents upends his physiology. Prolonged separations can even be fatal to an immature nervous system, as vital rhythms of heart rate and respiration devolve into chaos. Sudden infant death is increased fourfold in the babies of mothers who are depressed — because without emotional shelter, infants die. The heart rhythms of securely attached babies are steadier than those with insecure relationships, just as the breathing teddy bear regularizes the respiration of premature infants.

Being well regulated in relatedness is the deeply gratifying state that people seek ceaselessly in romance, religions, and cults; in husbands and wives, pets, softball teams, bowling leagues, and a thousand other features of human life driven by the thirst for sustaining affiliations.

Study after study has shown that children with close familial ties are far less likely to become entangled in substance abuse. Even under ideal circumstances, teenage years abound in emotional surges, changing roles, growing pains. If adolescents do not receive limbic stability from relationships in the home, they will be measurably more susceptible to chemical options outside.

We add video games to the list of potentially addictive options to which children may turn when they do not feel secure in a network of strong, regulating relationships. Our experience has shown us that multiplayer video games fill such a void *more powerfully* than other types of video games. The multiplayer games involve on-line and live chat, which, in the authors' opinion, heighten the illusion that gaming can satisfy the player's hunger to affiliate. What they do need is attachment that can exist in real time, in real proximity to others. We need to see, hear, touch, and smell one another; we need to ask for a hug or help with a move; we need to feel the loving energy of the ones we love. A Cyber community, without physical contact, cannot provide these things. This, we believe, is one reason why research has shown a strong correlation between the amount of time spent on-line and depression.

Relationships built through gaming vary greatly in the degree to which the players know one another outside the game.

Kelly was a gamer who played with friends he made at college, along with strangers he met in the game world. He discovered, over time, that it was hard to relate to his friends in any other way, particularly as his world became narrowly concentrated in the game. There was less and less dialogue with them beyond gaming because he did little else. As he became more and more addicted, he only met these friends on-line. Now that he is trying to reengage with the real world, some of these friends (the ones who are not addicted gamers) are delighted to see him again.

Todd was a gamer who concluded that friendships with gamers will usually last only as long as the players are playing together (unless a sexual and romantic on-line relationship springs up between players and is brought into real life). Todd found that when a player is absent from the community for more than a few weeks, he is unlikely to find "old friends" any more. He has no real names, no real addresses, and no phone numbers. Puff. Gone. He found that although real-life issues may get discussed to some extent, on-line gaming friends cannot be counted on beyond the moment or beyond the game. When a gamer quits a game, he quits that community. Todd, like other gamers, knew and accepted this about the on-line communities, yet he felt intensely attached to it. He had no other.

If your children have reached a point where their *Cyber* relationships are more important to them than *actual* relationships, then you have reason to be alarmed. These youths will fight hard to keep their Cyber communities, which means staying with the games and the chat. We have seen in our work with teenagers and young adults that when parents finally bring an end to the obsessive gaming, their children feel most upset about losing their on-line contacts and the sense of community that they have loved and in which they felt valued. Gamers know that once they stop gaming, many of those friendships will fall away.

The *lucky ones* have on-line friendships that will continue off-line, and these will have a better time weathering the withdrawal phase of gaming addiction. The *unlucky ones* face a frightening and lonely void when gaming and its associated community is taken away. These gamers are probably at greatest risk for violence and self-harm, so care must be taken to get them into counseling and, ideally, a therapy group and a real-life community where they can begin to build real-life friendships. We cover the topic of a formal intervention in Chapter 9 and we suggest you read it before taking action.

In conclusion, we believe that the strength of a person's conscience is influenced by the strength of a person's experience of growing up loved. You, the parents, must understand this so you will make the building of close family ties your first priority and limit your children's video gaming (and other screen time). Don't let anything interfere with the development of healthy ties to family and a real-life community.

If your child has become addicted to video games, there is something we would like you to remember. An addict's first loyalty is to the *beloved* (alcohol, cocaine, sex, romance, food, gambling, work, video gaming). Addiction puts an addict's conscience *to sleep*, which is why addicts behave in ways that they would never behave if not addicted. Their attachments to people become weaker than their attachments to the addiction, so they do not feel the expected remorse when they manipulate, lie, steal, assault, and cheat. These same people, once recovered from their addiction, often feel tremendous remorse for what they did while addicted. Their conscience starts to work once again and points the way toward appropriate behavior. The stronger their affiliations were to family and friends before they became addicted, the stronger will be their prick of conscience afterwards.

However, just because a person desires to do the right thing does not mean that he knows what the right thing is.

Developing a Moral Compass

The Internet infrastructure was originally intended to provide political and military communications in the event of war and other disasters. The World Wide Web, which uses the Internet infrastructure for non-military purposes, is intentionally designed to provide an open digital environment to everyone with the ability to access it. Monitoring, which does occur, is driven by a variety of objectives, like keeping it an open and accessible medium (i.e., free from malicious and illegal hacking), supporting the common good (e.g., free enterprise, scientific knowledge, political discourse, news and commentary, special interest groups, etc.), and, of course, protecting national security. Rules based on social norms have not yet been worked out for the Web, and so Websites can contain digital content that would be banned or physically controlled in the real world.

Different on-line communities have different norms for good and bad behavior, but, taken as a whole, anything can be found through the Internet. If, for example, you are curious about or drawn to antisocial behavior, it is easy to find hate groups, violence against women, child pornography, instructions on how to build bombs, etc. Video games span the moral spectrum. Increasing numbers of them allow and promote virtual antisocial behavior by making it a requirement for earning game points. In one popular game, Grand Theft Auto, the player can engage in antisocial behaviors such as theft and assault to earn points. The player can have virtual sex with a prostitute and then murder her! Many of the popular games require some form of thievery and/or assault in order to win. And not just military-style games, either. We are talking about games whose sole aim is to promote antisocial behavior. One such game principally involves massacring people with a chainsaw. Some of these games have been banned from some countries (Ireland and New Zealand, for instance).

Imagine if you will the experience of the child who is repeatedly rewarded in a game for the very behavior that is punished at home and at school. The younger a child is when they begin such game play, the greater their confusion. An adult who plays these games for the first time already has a fully developed (we hope) set of moral principles, and is therefore not confused so easily. But the shakier the sense of morality in that adult, the more susceptible they will be to the antisocial influences of the games.

Now, imagine a child who does not yet have a strong grasp of moral and ethical behavior. As will be discussed in later chapters, this clarity develops over a whole childhood. Training in moral behavior, like any other training, involves a child successfully making synaptic connections that are deep enough to provide moral structure to the brain. If a child receives consistent messages, that child will not be confused. But if the child is playing a lot of video games with messages that go against his family's values, then this child is much more likely to be mixed up about right and wrong. When you add TV to the mix, children may be spending many hours learning the very behaviors their parents and teachers want to discourage.

Parents can minimize the confusion by being consistent in their messages about moral behavior, modeling it for their children, and minimizing their children's exposure to video games (and TV shows) that are inconsistent with this message. When situations are presented, even in sitcoms where the behaviors displayed are antithetical to a family's values, parents might consider using those occasions as *teachable moments* to engage their children in a conversation that addresses the issues of concern (after the program is over). This will help the child's brain develop the structures that support moral behavior.

We would like to end this discussion of conscience and morality by noting the power of video games to overcome the natural inhibition that humans feel about killing others. This natural inhibition has meant that throughout human history, military leaders have been frustrated by their soldiers' unwillingness to kill the enemy. It has been estimated that the vast majority of soldiers would not aim to kill — until recently, that is. Now, thanks to practice with video games, the percentages are reversed. In fact, America's armed forces have gone into the business of making games for recruitment and training.

Most might consider this to be an appropriate strategy for the military; it is, after all, in the business of killing the enemy. But think about the implications of this. These are the same games that our children are playing. It really is no surprise that the children who went on a killing rampage at Columbine High School were players of violent video games. The context for that killing was complex, so the killing spree cannot be laid solely at the feet of that violent game (bullying at school and uninvolved parents were also key factors). However, Doom, the game that those two boys had been playing for years, appears to have entered their consciousness to such a degree that they truly felt themselves to be living inside the game. Jerald Block, a psychiatrist who has made a careful investigation of the e-mails and other records left behind by the boys, finds clear evidence for a blurring of reality and game fantasy.

Self-Confidence and Social Skills

Limiting screen time and providing children with the healthy environment that they need allows them to develop emotionally and socially. Later chapters provide details about what children need at each developmental stage. Here, we want only to give a broad picture of the negative impact that unlimited or untimely gaming can have on the developing child's self-confidence and social skills.

Ironically, many gamers claim that the self-esteem they enjoy is directly the result of their gaming skills. Indeed, among themselves, status in the social hierarchy of the game is determined by skill level, as well as social behavior within their Cyber communities. This is part of why they resist so strongly any parental attempt to limit access to this source of self-esteem. The question is: how stable and robust is this self-esteem? Will it sustain a gamer who is no longer gaming? Does it provide enough self-confidence that a gamer will be able to embrace adult life with self-assurance?

Our experience with video game addicts is that their self-esteem is, in fact, extremely fragile. When the aforementioned Kelly came for counseling, he had no confidence in his ability to do anything in the real world. Even though he was running out of money, he avoided looking for work, believing that he could not find a job. His flunking out of college left him feeling guilty and incompetent. He avoided people and felt unlikable, unworthy, and unsuccessful. He was a skilled gamer, having achieved recognition within that community for his prowess. But this success did little to help him in the real world, where he felt paralyzed with fear. He did not have Asperger's syndrome. He simply lacked the synaptic connections in his brain that would correspond to the skills he needed to live life competently.

Now twenty-four, he is learning to feel good about himself. He now has a job and is making plans to move to a better apartment. Once he develops his social skills and has some success in that arena, his self-esteem will get a big boost. When he either returns to and finishes college or lands a good job without a college degree, his self-esteem will begin to soar. If, however, he stays hidden behind his computer screen, venturing no farther than the safe Cyber world he knows so well, his self-esteem will never develop into something robust that will be able to sustain him throughout a normal life, with all of its challenges.

Casey

Casey was a sixteen-year-old boy who loved to play on-line Halo. He had no interests outside of gaming. He maintained good grades in school, but during the summer he played Halo up to ten hours a day. All of his social life happened on-line. He rarely left the house. Although he was old enough to drive, he had no interest in getting a driver's license. His mother did not require him to do any chores around the house. His one obligation was to go to bed by midnight. Since she went to bed two hour earlier, there was no way she could enforce the midnight rule.

Casey's self-esteem derived from two sources: gaming and school grades. Because of how he lived his life, he lacked competence in many areas that would be considered normal for his age. He did not know how to cook, clean, drive, work, shop, or handle money. He was immature and his self-esteem was low. The amount of time he spent gaming during the summer break got him hooked into an addictive pattern that he was not able to break once school began. As a result, Casey's grades suffered, as did his self-esteem. He needed to have his gaming severely curtailed and be taught the basics of self-care. He needed to become a responsible, contributing member of his family. And he needed to be supported as he socialized outside the family. Since his mother did not seem to recognize what her son required, she needed her own education and support to make changes. Her son was resistant, but without such changes, his prospects were poor.

Pro-Social Behavior

Research has shown two important sources of self-esteem in children: competencies and pro-social behavior. We have been discussing competencies or the lack thereof among children who game extensively. We now turn our attention to *pro-social behavior*. This term refers to the ability of children to get along well with others. Again, later chapters discuss this in greater depth. Here, we simply want the reader to understand that children with good social skills, who do get along well with others, have much better self-esteem than those who do not.

What parents need to understand is that a child who spends the majority of free time gaming and doing other things on the Internet is not developing social skills that readily apply to the real world. Good social skills need social interaction in the real world in order to develop thoroughly. Research long ago determined that *nonverbal* communication is actually much more powerful than *verbal* communication. People place greater confidence in how they read nonverbal messages.

For example, if a person frowns, but says she is happy, we will not believe they are happy. So, to be an effective communicator, a child must learn how to send and read these nonverbal messages correctly. Typed communication is purely verbal. On-line writers have evolved symbols designed to communicate the intended emotion behind what has been typed (so-called *emoticons*), but this remains a poor substitute for the non-verbal, energetic reality of face-to-face communication. Even telephone communication, while richer than typed communication, lacks a non-verbal dimension.

There is simply no way around it. If you want your children to be highly effective communicators, who can connect comfortably with others, handle conflict well, and enter the adult world with the skills they need for interpersonal success, we urge you to limit their on-line time according to the guidelines provided here. Some on-line socializing can benefit children's social skills and attendant self-esteem, but, once again, it is up to you, the parents, to monitor this, making sure the time spent is not detracting from the real-life experiences needed by all children.

Are There Benefits?

As we have already stated, it is the *excesses* of video gaming that concern us. If parents follow our guidelines, then their children should be able to enjoy video games without adverse effects. Their brains and bodies will be able to develop normally. Do video games offer real benefits? That is debatable and we will leave it to parents to decide for themselves. Certainly, children want to fit in with their peers, so knowing and being able to play video games meets that need in children.

Video games are a powerful medium. The best of them allow players to learn skills and lessons through the right combination of challenge and reward. There are games designed to teach specific lessons or skills and there are games designed for entertainment. The best teaching games are entertaining. James Paul Gee, in his book, *What Video Games Must Teach Us about Learning and Literacy,* believes that good video games can be "life enhancing." He describes several games that he has played and enumerates the many learning principles involved and the many benefits that he believes accrue through their play, such as experiencing different points of view, being made to look at our unquestioned assumptions, and so forth.

We do not disagree with him. We do, however, think that parents need to exercise control over what games they allow their children to play and for how long. Because many games are highly challenging, rewarding, and time-consuming, and because children are children, it is unrealistic to think that kids will limit themselves.

Video gaming is reported to be of benefit in developing certain kinds of fine-motor, hand-eye coordination. There are reports that surgeons, for example, find it helpful to play certain video games before surgery. We mentioned earlier in this chapter the benefits that the military has found in games that help with combat training. Video games are being developed for other training purposes, as well. Parents of children with special needs may already have found games that are helping their children develop specific skills. There are serious game developers who want to harness the power of gaming for many educational purposes. Games for Change is the name of one such group. We encourage parents to follow what they and similar groups are doing.

Many games are touted by marketers as being educational without evidence that they actually are. We advise you do your own thorough investigation before you accept such claims. If you allow some gaming in your home, due diligence must be done to limit it to games that you believe are truly life enhancing.

3
Setting Limits: It's Just a Game

Taking away the video game seems to have become the most common punishment in American households today. This typically leads to power struggles, and even elevates that prized gaming device in a child's eyes. Just imagine how literacy rates would increase if children had to earn back their favorite Harry Potter or Nancy Drew book. Setting limits with children and teens about their use of electronic entertainment can be a daunting task. Many parents know that they need to set limits but are unsure about how to start the process. Others have tried repeatedly and given up in frustration.

How much time on the computer is appropriate for my child? How much gaming is too much? What games are OK? When should he play on the computer? These are the questions that most parents struggle with when deciding on rules for their child's computer use. It often comes down to creating a healthy balance by establishing rules that help your child develop a well-rounded lifestyle. Is he doing well in most areas? Is there room in her schedule for homework, sports, or exercise, time with family and friends? Is your child exhibiting any signs of gaming misuse or addiction?

Children thrive in environments with established routines. They gain a sense of security in knowing what is going to happen in their day. And surprisingly, they also appreciate rules and a parent who is consistent in sticking to them. Your twelve-year-old may not thank you for holding him accountable after he has violated curfew, but at age twenty-five he'll appreciate your dedication to his well-being. So even though the act of setting and enforcing limits on your child's gaming will no doubt lead to some conflict, it is essential that she learn to effectively balance her own use of technology, and that starts with the limits you set.

Many parents say that they are afraid to provoke their children. Alice, mother of seven-year-old Sam, refused to take away his Game Boy any more. "The tantrums he throws are awful; I just don't want to deal with it!" Sam has thrown his Game Boy at his mother — once hitting her on the back of the head while she was driving. "He screams and yells, throws himself on the floor at the grocery store, beats his fists against the wall...I have learned to just let him keep the thing. At least when he is playing he is quiet."

Alice and many other parents cite their fear as a barrier to setting limits on their children's gaming. In the above example, Alice allows her son to effectively bully her into getting what he wants. Sam, in turn, uses this learned behavior to harass the kids at his daycare in order to play with his favorite toys, to be the team leader in softball games, or to get the biggest serving of pretzels at snack time. He doesn't keep friends for very long, and this doesn't seem to bother him. He usually gets what he wants.

Seventeen-year-old Evan was addicted to an on-line game called EverQuest. His parents, Deb and Carl, struggled with this problem for years. Their pattern was to set a limit, but not to follow through with any significant consequence. Evan announced that he was dropping out of high school. The school had already threatened to expel him because he had accumulated too many absences. He told his parents that he was too tired from being up all night gaming to go to school anymore. His parents viewed this as the final straw, rallied their strength, and decided to remove the computer from their son's room. Evan's response was violent. He punched holes in his bedroom walls, kicked down his door, and threatened to leave and never speak to them again. He challenged them, "Do you want me to live on the streets, because that's just what I will do!" The next day his computer was returned to his room.

Will seven-year-old Sam, with his behavior problem and antisocial tendencies, grow up to become like seventeen-year-old Evan with a gaming addiction, antisocial behavior, no high school diploma, and no prospects?

Our children depend upon us to determine fair limits and to set these limits for them; it is not a skill that they can develop without teaching and experience. As adults, we understand the difficulties in trying to maintain balance. We complain often about not having enough hours in the day and of feeling "burned out." We give our sons and daughter a tremendous head start in life by teaching them that healthy limits means respecting the integrity of their family.

The following section offers a step-by-step guide to setting limits. Carefully consider your own choices before beginning this process with your child. In addition to your task of enforcing these rules, you will be looked upon as a role model. If you are the parent of an older child or teen, expect your own gaming behavior to be scrutinized. Parents need to be willing to look closely at their own gaming habits and act as role models for their children. This does not mean that parents and children need to adhere to exactly the same rules. However, it is vital that family members operate within a similar philosophy. Credibility is fundamental to parental authority.

Step One: Setting Yourself up for Success

The electronic entertainment industry is still relatively young. Educators, psychologists, and child development specialists have been conducting and reviewing research for the past ten years to help families make informed decisions about computer gaming. We are now at a point where there are some basic, agreed-upon guidelines:

o   No screen time for children under two years of age.
o   One to two hours of daily screen time for preschool-aged children.
o   Two hours for elementary-aged children.
o   Two to three hours of daily screen time for middle- and high-school-aged teens.
o   Screen time means both television and computer entertainment.
o   No television, Internet, or gaming console in your child's room.

Consistency is the key to effectiveness when it comes to setting limits with your children. There are three main threats to consistency:

o   One is setting a limit that you are not willing or able to enforce.

o The second is setting a limit that all parental figures in your household don't agree upon.

o The third is setting a limit that is unfair. If the limit is unfair, you will feel guilty, your child will feel hurt, and the limit will not be enforced with consistency.

If you are serious about these limits, ensure your success by agreeing on a plan with your parenting partner ahead of time. It is important for couples to discuss their concerns openly and reach agreement before approaching their child. Often men and women have different perspectives about the role and function of the computer in their home. It has been our experience that men tend to be less concerned about the negative impact of computer gaming. Often they can better relate to the sense of pleasure that is gained from playing first-person shooter games, as they themselves are the primary buyers of them.

Typically, it is the mother who makes first contact with a counselor to express concern about her child's gaming. It is the mother who finds herself stressed out and exhausted from the power struggles with her child over a game. And, while many fathers have similar concerns, a large number seem to minimize any potentially harmful effects and make excuses for their child's desire for more game time. If you and your partner have conflicted views on gaming, now is the time to reach a compromise.

Carol told fifteen-year-old Jay that he had to stop gaming by 10 PM on school nights and by midnight on the weekend. Jay routinely ignored this rule and often gamed until 3 or 4 in the morning. He usually slept through his morning classes and didn't arrive at school until noon. Carol was shocked when the school counselor called to discuss his absenteeism. She worked from 6 AM – 3 PM as a nurse at the local hospital. She fell asleep by 9 PM and was out of the house at 5:30 AM. She has assumed that her son was abiding by her computer rules. He had always been a trustworthy child. She had set a rule that she was not capable of enforcing.

Are your limits enforceable? Will you be available to follow through with a consequence if a rule is violated? While you may have the best intentions, this is the time to be real about your own boundaries. One way to do this is to use a timer. When the timer goes off, your child's media time is up, no exceptions. There are several software programs that can assist parents enforce time limits on gaming. "PC Moderator" is an example of a hardware product that allows parents to set time limits on computer gaming. When the allotted amount of time has been used, the computer will shut down. The manufacturers know that in many households children have greater technical skills than their parents. So this hardware is designed to be easily implemented by parents, and not so easily hacked by tech-savvy kids.

What do children and teens view as fair limits? Most complain that their parents have no idea about what kind of game they are playing. They want their parents to consider the structure of their game when setting limits. Some games can be paused and saved. Some have time limits intrinsic to their program. Other games, like the massive multi-player on-line role-playing games (MMORPGs), are interactive and are based on scenarios that are unpredictable. These games contain the most addictive characteristics and pose the greatest challenge for parents and players alike. For example, fifteen-year-old Pete loves playing Counter-strike and once he begins a gaming session he likes to have ninety minutes to complete it. Because it is a combat game that requires teams, he may have other people counting on him to achieve their goal. Pete's mother didn't know any of this when she walked into his room and told him to be off the computer in five minutes. He whined and complained while she became angrier. Then she found herself yelling at the back of her son's head. Pete lost his temper. He ended up being grounded from the computer for two weeks. He assumed that his mother was cruel. He didn't think that he could talk to her about anything important. If Pete and his mother had communicated about the game ahead of time, they could have reached a compromise that left them both feeling respected and happy.

Once you have decided on fair limits for your family's gaming and Internet use, once you have reached an agreement with your spouse or parenting partner and ensured that you can enforce these limits, you are ready for step two.

Step Two: The Family Meeting

The family meeting is an excellent parenting tool for families that have children aged eight and older. They are best when they happen in a warm and friendly environment where each family member is offered the opportunity to be heard. Far from formal, these meetings need to be casual and relaxed. As a parent, never come to a family meeting in anger. It is not a forum for discipline. It is a means of improving and enhancing your cohesiveness as a family. The family meeting provides the structure for listening, understanding, and bonding. It is an excellent place to begin a discussion about gaming and the use of electronic entertainment.

The Family Meeting Agenda

o   Make a gaming plan. Just as you would for other activities, schedule gaming times and choices in advance. A gaming plan helps everyone choose and use gaming carefully. This is also the time to address *fairness* issues with siblings. Don't worry about setting different rules for your ten-year-old and your sixteen-year-old.

o Set time limits. Limit children's total screen time. This includes time playing video and computer games and surfing the Internet. You may also wish to include television viewing.

o Set family guidelines for gaming content. Help children and teens choose video games that are appropriate for their ages and interests. Get into the habit of checking the content ratings and parental advisories for all media. Use these ratings to help you to decide which media are suitable for your child.

o Be clear and consistent with children about media rules. If you do not approve of their media choice, explain why and help them choose something more appropriate. If you don't know what your child is playing, ask questions and learn about your child's favorite games. Know what he is playing. Offer to sit in on a session to better understand the nature of his experience and to witness his behavior. Try playing the game a few times on your own. Note the language and gaming slang.

o Develop and follow up on consequences.

o Develop a list of other things to do that are fun. This is a good time to remind the group that gaming is a *leisure* activity. It is entertainment. Don't make the common mistake of reducing game time and assuming that your child will know what to do with himself. Developing a list of enjoyable activities that can fill the void is a positive way to conclude your family meeting. The most common reason children cite for playing both console and hand-held games is boredom. If you expect this extra time to be filled with chores or homework, your child will feel cheated. Surprisingly, most teens and children will happily trade solitary game time for joining in fun activities that involve friends or family. Often this means that parents must restructure their own time, as they spend more one-on-one time with their children. If your child's gaming time has given you some much needed "down time," consider revising some priorities and delegating tasks as a means of maintaining your own personal sense of balance. Maybe the dirty dishes stay longer in the sink or the grass doesn't get mowed as often. Say to others, "Sorry, I can't do that right now. I'm busy playing with my child."

o   Schedule the next family meeting. Once a month is ideal. Let family members know that they are welcome to request a family meeting at any time.

When the authors think about the power of play, we think of thirteen-year-old Jack, who once entered our office with a scowl. "What's going on, Jack?" asked the counselor. "I don't know...can we just play cards?" During that card game, Jack spoke about one of his friends, a girl who cuts herself on her arm, and shared his worries. By the end of the card game he had a plan for dealing with the situation, asking for help, and which adults to involve. Play is the language of children and it offers psychological benefits to family members of any age.

Step Three: Logical Consequences

You have already decided upon gaming rules and communicated these rules to your children. The next step is to *pre-determine* logical consequences. Below is a list of our recommendations. In the spirit of consistency, take some time to discuss these with all household members who will have the power to enforce your rules.

*Age: **Under five***
First misuse: Time out and a parent-child talk.
Second misuse: Time out and a parent-child talk.
Third misuse: Remove the game.

Children in this age group have difficulty tracking the passage of time. If, after two reminders, your child is not following your rules about game usage, then it is best to take the game away. Doing so will save you many future power struggles. Making an agreement with your child about earning the game back sends the message that the game is a highly valuable possession, which may not be a good tactic. Rather, tell your child that the game isn't right for the family at this time. Let it go, introduce other fun activities, and your child will likely forget about games, at least for a while.

*Age: **Five to eleven years old***
First misuse: Time out and a parent-child talk.
Second misuse: Time out, a parent-child talk, and no gaming for remainder of the day.
Third misuse: Time out, a parent-child talk, and no gaming for the weekend.
Fourth misuse: Time out, a parent-child talk, no gaming for a week, and a discussion about losing all gaming privileges.
Fifth misuse: Loss of all gaming privileges for at least one month. At that time, parent and child must come to an agreement about proper usage before gaming will be permitted.

School-age children will benefit from these logical consequences. The more you consistently follow through with the consequences, the less likely you will repeat it. Children in this age group will push and test their parent's limits. So if you take computer games away for a week, don't give in early — even if your daughter washes your car or has a birthday coming up. Show your appreciation for her kindness, but follow through with the consequence you set. If you don't follow through, your child will begin to view your threats as meaningless and lose respect for your authority. Intermittent reinforcement works in reverse. If the child occasionally succeeds in getting the parent to give in, the next time the child's effort will be even stronger.

Age: Thirteen to eighteen years old

First misuse: Time out and a parent-child talk.

Second misuse: Time out, a parent-child talk, and no gaming for remainder of the day.

Third misuse: Time out, a parent-child talk, no gaming for the weekend, and a family meeting. At this meeting, explore options: remove the computer from the bedroom, discontinue the Internet, install time limit software, and stop subscription for MMORPGs.

Fourth misuse: Time out, parent-child talk, and enforce the consequence established at family meeting.

Fifth misuse: Loss of all gaming privileges for an indefinite period of time. Resumption of gaming only after parent and child have come to an agreement. If an agreement is reached, and the child later violates its terms, gaming is never permitted again.

Generally, older teens know exactly what their responsibilities are. They require less repetition of the rules but more patience with their response to a consequence. Emotions are strong and typically fragile. Teens often respond impulsively and don't have the best emotional control. Don't be surprised if your teen tries to pick a fight with you while you are trying to enforce a consequence. Teens are very adept at knowing how to push their parents "buttons." So the key here is to remain focused on your task, no matter how hard your teen tries to divert you. Now is not the time to respond to their incendiary comments.

Step Four: Enforcement

Enforcement is your final step. If you have followed the processes described in this chapter, you may find yourself surprised by how well this goes. The structure of enforcement is fairly easy. The language of enforcement looks like this:

- o　Give your direction.
- o　Repeat your direction.
- o　Repeat a second time; add a consequence.
- o　Follow through.

Example: Young child

Parent:　Time's up, time to log off.

Child:　-no response-

Parent:　(approaches child and makes eye contact) I said time is up, it is time to log off.

Child:　Ah, come on, can't I play for five more minutes … pleeeeeeeeese.

Parent:　No, I said that time is up. Log off or their will be a consequence.

Child:　(ignores and keeps playing)

Parent: OK, I told you to log off and you have not, so I will do it for you. (Turns off or unplugs the computer, walks away, and does not engage in argument.)

Example: School-aged child

Parent: Time's up, time to log off.

Child: But mom, we just reached this really cool dungeon. Can't I play longer?

Parent: Time's up, log off. Remember, we agreed.

Child: I know but can't I just play a little longer? I won't play tomorrow if I can stay on longer.

Parent: No, I said that time is up. Log off or there will be a consequence.

Child: OK.

Example: Middle school-aged teen

Parent: Time's up, time to log off.

Child: OK.

Parent: (remains next to child waiting) I said that it is time to log off. Remember, we agreed.

Child: I will. (still playing)

Parent: I said that time is up. Log off or there will be a consequence.

Child: I said OK, I will! (still playing)

Parent: OK, I told you to log off and you have not, so I will do it for you. (Turns off or unplugs the computer, walks away, and does not engage in argument.)

Example: High school-aged teen

Parent: Time's up. Time to log off.

Child: No way that it has already been two hours.

Parent: I said that it is time to log off. And, yes, it has been two hours.

Child: This sucks.

Parent: I said that time is up. Log off or there will be a consequence.

Child: Fine! This place is the pits. I can't wait to move out and live on my own!

Parent: Sorry you feel that way (or some other non-inflammatory one-liner). Parent disengages and walks away.

The Cool-Down Period

If your interaction with your child during enforcement was stressful or marked by a strong emotional reaction, send him to his room for a cool-down period. This will benefit both of you. Let him know that you will be in to talk with him in ten to twenty minutes, depending on age. Give older children and teens twenty minutes to cool down, younger children a shorter amount of time. Consider how long it will take you to calm down and be ready to communicate in a healthy manner.

When you talk to your child, listen to his feelings; *but do not engage in compromises about your limits*. These limits on gaming had already been established and should be no surprise. If your child has a strong gripe about the limit, let him know that he can talk about it at the next family meeting. Changes will not be made right now. Remind him that the game is an extra activity and that you expect time limits to be respected in the future.

If you followed the above steps and found that you were unsuccessful, it is probably time to seek professional support. There may be contributing factors that need attention. Children with ADHD, learning disabilities, mood disorders, addiction issues, or anger management problems pose unique parenting challenges. Professional services from school counselors, psychologists, social workers, or family therapists can evaluate your family's needs, and help direct you to the appropriate resources.

4
Infants and Toddlers (Birth to 2 years old)

Tony and Emily were like many first time parents. They both were well-educated and had spent their lives as young adults focusing on building their careers and enjoying life. They met and married in their early thirties. Feeling the pressure of a ticking biological clock, Emily was eager to get pregnant and begin building a family. Along with the pregnancy came a focus on researching the best possible options for their child. Many books were purchased as Emily monitored her diet and exercise. Tony read books out loud to his unborn son in bed at night. They both felt a strong desire to raise their child the "correct way" and to ensure that he had all of the advantages.

When Jared was born, they continued this pursuit of excellence on his behalf. Wanting their son to have an advantage, they exposed him to *lapwear* (educational software designed especially for babies). The couple firmly believed in a philosophy of "the earlier the better."

Lapware is a growing trend in personal computer software with programs aimed at a new market: six-month-old babies through the toddler age. Lapware is for toddlers who sit on the lap of a caregiver. Most designed-for-babies software allows children to either tap the keys on the keyboard in a random manner for an onscreen reaction, or to deliberately swipe the mouse without a need for clicking.

Consider a recent print advertisement from the manufacturer of a keyboard designed for one year olds:

> *An attractive 25-year-old woman with blond hair and blue eyes sits in a chair facing her home computer system. On her lap is a round, fair-haired baby boy. Both are smiling and seem to be happily focused on the screen.*

What might be wrong with such a seemingly pleasant scene?

First, we need to consider the developmental tasks of the infant. Birth through age one is the critical period when children learn to establish trust. During this first year of life, infants depend on others for food, warmth, and affection, and must be able to blindly trust their caregivers. If their needs are met consistently and responsively, infants not only will develop a secure attachment with their caregiver but will also learn to trust their environment in general. If not, infants will develop mistrust towards people and things in their environment, even towards themselves.

A recent study published in the *Journal of Pediatrics* found that, among babies aged eight months to sixteen months, every daily hour spent watching programs such as Brainy Baby or Baby Einstein translated into six to eight fewer words in their vocabularies as compared with other children their age. Yet, in the most recent survey by the Kaiser Family Foundation (June 2007), 56 percent of parents report that they believe that baby videos have a positive effect on their child's development.

Human beings are highly social creatures. Our brains are designed to be in relationship with other people. Interactive communication shapes both the structure and function of the brain. Brain researchers report that the attachment experience is directly responsible for activating or not activating a child's genetic potential. What infants need most is social interaction and physical contact with their caregivers.

The Computer Screen: A Cold Caretaker

Bonding is the most meaningful psychosocial process known to humans. No single factor has a more far-reaching influence in the development of our psyches. Through the natural bonding process, we develop the abilities to attach and to trust. Secure attachment establishes the basis on which the child will form relationships with others — his sense of security about exploring the world, his resilience to stress, his ability to balance his emotions, make sense of his life, and create meaningful interpersonal relationships in the future.

The sense of touch translates into feelings of safety, security, and love. *Facing a computer to read a story is not the same as facing a parent whose physical warmth and expressions of love and excitement help create a trusting and secure environment.* Developmental psychologist David Elkind makes clear his opinion that computers are not benign tools, but actually can be quite harmful to the child. He states:

An even more serious side effect of such programming is their potentially harmful impact upon the parent-child relationship.... Lapware [thus] has the potential for impairing the child's sense of trust and security that are essential for the infant to explore his world with pleasure and confidence.

His insights, coupled with our own observations, prompt us to ask: Are we raising a new generation of children who are bonding with artificial parents?

For the toddler, age one to two, it is all about autonomy. Toddlers learn to walk, talk, use utensils, and do things for themselves. Their self-control and self-confidence begin to develop at this stage. If we provide too many stimulating options to toddlers, if we give them access to computer games with their many bright, colorful, alluring choices, we find that they may not be able to keep up. If we encourage their use of initiative to explore their world and offer reassurance when mistakes are made, children will develop the confidence needed to cope with future situations that require choice, control, and independence. We offer this reassurance in many ways — *verbally*, with supportive words; *physically*, with a hand on the shoulder; and *emotionally*, with a compassionate look and a moment of eye contact. There is no value in the introduction of a computer game that renders judgment of success or failure with a flashing icon and canned applause at a stage in life when *they are really learning what it means to be human* and navigate in the real world.

Some parents have noted that their very young children often develop relationships with the characters in computer games and experience confusion when categorizing them as alive or not alive. Jean Piaget, a founder of modern child psychology, noted that the child at this stage has an active imagination and vivid fantasies. It is not uncommon for him to personify objects and ascribe will and intention to inanimate phenomena. Children are especially likely to perceive animate qualities in toys that have living counterparts (teddy bears, dolls, and action figures). Smart toys are increasingly socially interactive, which increases the likelihood that children will form stronger attachments with them than with traditional toys such as a teddy bear.

Today's children are the victims of a new world order that accommodates machines such as computers and intelligent toys. Children are negotiating territory that many adults have yet to explore — the blurring of boundaries between the living and the mechanical. This represents what amounts to performing an unintended scientific experiment on our children, one that may reap unknown and unanticipated consequences in the future, not all of which may be benign.

Remember that children must first acquire rich, natural sensory experiences and knowledge. Avoid premature exposure to the artificial world of computers without the necessary prior understanding to make sense of what they see on a screen. Do not add to their confusion; they are too young to be placed in front of computer screens.

Are parents placing so much value on children's proficiency with computers that they risk overlooking the importance of other kinds of educational experiences? Disney sells its mouse-eared, child-friendly version of a desktop computer called the Dream Desk PC. And many a tech-savvy parent will purchase this computer for their young child with the belief that they are giving their child an advantage. However, if you look past the surface, it becomes clear that computers are replacing vital parent-child interactions. *More screen time typically equals less social interaction.* Logically, the more the toddler or baby is interfacing with the computer, the less he or she is interacting with others. Technology and electronic entertainment put distance between young children and their caregivers.

Better Moral Development?

Will your child grow up to have the type of personality and character traits that you would hope for? Will she know right from wrong, have empathy and compassion for others, and believe in fairness? Will he be tolerant of others, be free of racial and gender prejudices, and treat people the way that he, in turn, would expect to be treated? Will technology become more influential in determining a child's morality than a grandparent?

We know that moral development begins in the first two years of life. At about eighteen months, children begin to understand when they have done something wrong; that is, done something that a caretaker or parent *believes* is right or wrong. We praise our children for acting well and redirect them when they are behaving badly at this early age. Moral teaching is, of course, limited and is communicated both through unconditional love and by physically showing our children how to act by doing things with them each day. According to Michael Gurian, author of *The Good Son,*

> *...both moral training and the lack of it depend on "the sacred world" — the home and other intimate environments we create for our infant... We can only hurt his moral development by letting him be exposed to things we consider amoral or immoral — most of these would come to him through media and video games.*

Parents should be aware that many computer games promote violence or negative social, racial, or gender stereotypes. Young children who see violent acts in movies, shows, and games may not be able to tell the difference between "make-believe" and real life. They may not understand that *real* violence hurts and kills people. When the "good guys" or heroes use violence, children may learn that it is OK to use force to solve problems. Younger children may even become more afraid of the world around them.

It is easy to see the obvious negativity associated with playing excessively violent games. What isn't so apparent is the influence of the seemingly benign screen images. Clip art is a good example of a collection of graphics that has become so commonplace in our Cyber world that it often lurks below our radar. A century ago, clip art was limited to chaste books that provided consumers with an abundance of copyright-free art they could immediately publish. The use of clip art in the computer age is widespread throughout most educational and business environments. It has been included in the educational materials children will use from kindergarten through college, and can be found on parent-child oriented Websites and software. Clip art has evolved into the complex computer graphics that are used in today's games.

A research study that appeared in the academic journal *Sex Roles: A Journal of Research* examined the cultural impact of clip art images. The researchers concluded that the use of clip art is likely to encourage traditional gender schemas in viewers. Here are some of their findings:

- o Images of middle-aged males with light complexions were far more common than any other type.
- o Males were depicted in more diverse and active/nonnurturant roles than females. Illustrations depicted males in predominantly nonnurturant behaviors, in which they were physically mobile or producing some product.
- o Females were more likely to be depicted as teenagers.
- o Females were also shown with more revealing wardrobes (such as bathing suits, short dresses, short shorts, and short skirts), which means that females were more likely to be drawn with their legs bare.

o Females were more likely to be portrayed in passive positions, or delegated to the role of "audience" (e.g., passively accompanying or observing a male). Females were also more likely to be shown in active nurturant activities such as feeding a baby or cleaning the kitchen.

These findings concur with other research on the media, which show that in clip art images, males are depicted in more prominent and powerful activities and that representations of women are more sexualized than those of men. It is easy to think that when businesses and schools are using these stereotypical images they could be negatively affecting the performance of women and minorities. But, as parents, we need to consider the impact of such seemingly innocent images on our children's perceptions of what it means to be male or female in this world. And, yes, we believe that even a one-year-old can be influenced by screen images.

Marketing for Infants and Toddlers

Video game makers have sold hundreds of millions of dollars' worth of video games to parents aiming to put their babies on the fast track.

According to the American Association of School Administrators, parents ranked computer literacy above social, relational, and emotional skills as a priority for their child's educational experience. Parents feel pressure to get their children on the computer as early as possible. This pressure comes from friends and family, software developers, game manufacturers, educators, and, perhaps most strongly, from their own belief that the earlier they introduce technology to the child, the more likely it is to provide a valuable experience that will have long-term benefits. There is a belief that learning to interface with the computer at an early age is similar to the benefits of learning how to read when very young.

Software manufacturers lure parents into spending their money on these games with two very attractive hooks: 1) educational benefits to the child; and 2) free time for the parent. The industry is banking on the fact that you can't say no to the purchase of a game that promises to give your child an intellectual advantage. Their marketing research indicates that parents of infants and toddlers are often exhausted and often feel rushed in their day-to-day life. Advertisers know that television time is often used to entertain baby while Mom or Dad grabs those few minutes to finish folding the clothes, answer a phone call, return an e-mail, or just take a deep breath.

The names of the some of the popular software include Brainy Baby, Kid Genius, Baby Einstein, JumpStart, Learning Center Series, and Educator's Series. Each challenges infants to match shapes and colors in a variety of vivid formats. All describe themselves as educational tools that will give your baby an advantage over those other babies who don't play these games. But before you buy, consider our opinion that none of these games have been proven to have significant educational benefits.

Emerging literacy begins in infancy as a parent lifts a baby, looks into her eyes, and speaks softly to her. This pleasant interaction helps your baby learn about the flow of communication and the joy of conversing with others. Such interactions may seem trivial, but learning is taking place. Young children continue to develop listening and speaking skills as they communicate their needs and desires through sounds and gestures, babble to themselves and others, say their first words, and rapidly add new words to their spoken vocabularies.

Most children who have been surrounded by language from birth are fluent speakers by age three, regardless of intelligence, and without the aid of learning software. If you are concerned about giving your baby every possible advantage to stimulate his or her intellectual achievement, then be attentive to your baby's learning cues and follow his or her lead. Read and familiarize yourself with normal child development, provide opportunities for verbal interactions, provide safe objects to manipulate, respond to non-verbal communication, and be aware of fatigue. This is your *window of opportunity* to instill feelings of trust, safety, and security in your child. Learning will happen along the way.

What Parents Can Do

The following is a list of what parents can do to facilitate healthy bonding:

o Interact with your child in a style that includes all of the five senses (auditory, visual, touch, smell, and taste).

o Encourage the development of healthy attachments. Smile and look children in the eyes as you greet them. Spend time with the child. During this time, get on the floor, listen, and establish eye contact. Use touch to comfort or hold hands. Help children learn appropriate social/emotional language (how close to stand, how to use eye contact, when to touch, how to touch).

o Let your own self-care be important. There is wisdom in the adage "nurture the mother, nurture the child." When the parent is replenished, he or she is better able to parent in a healthy manner.

o Give your baby a variety of safe items of different shapes, sizes, and textures to explore, both indoors and outdoors.

o Wait until age two to introduce television. Do not introduce computer or video games to your baby or toddler. Be skeptical of educational or developmental claims made by advertisers, especially product claims of intellectual enhancement.

5
Early Childhood
(Ages 2 – 6)

I first noticed three-year-old Jessica playing her hand-held electronic game while she sat in my office reception area. She was waiting for her mother to fill out forms. She sat quietly in a chair with her eyes fixed on the screen. The paperwork took longer than anticipated so I went to check on Jessica. She remained sitting in the same chair and was still playing the game. When the forms were complete, I accompanied the mother to the waiting area to again find Jessica sitting in the same position.

I made the comment that twenty minutes is a long time for a three-year-old to sit so patiently. Her mother seemed pleased and told me that she always keeps this game handy when she needs her child to sit still. I then learned that the game was given to Jessica at home when her mother was working on her computer, or cooking a meal, or talking on the phone — or anytime when she did not want to be interrupted. It also accompanied Jessica on most car trips or medical appointments.

Early childhood is the time to encourage imaginative play with other children and provide interactive opportunities for mastery. It is the time when imaginary friends appear, profanity is repeated (even though its meaning is not known), and many children begin to feel afraid in the dark. Vocabulary develops rapidly along with a child's gross motor skills. It is often a stressful period for parents as they struggle to be consistent, set healthy boundaries, and navigate tantrums. Early preschoolers are not ready for abstract activities. *It is more important for the Jessicas of the world to pet a dog than to manipulate a video image of one.*

Tantrums and Aggressive Behavior

Mention the phrase "terrible twos" to a group of parents of preschool-age children and watch everyone nod in an empathetic acknowledgement that this is an especially challenging developmental period. Parents of two-year-olds often spend a lot of time saying *no* and redirecting their child's behavior. It is often a period marked with aggression and tantrums. Again, your child's task is to control impulses and learn to respect boundaries and limitations. Parents struggle to stop the hitting, kicking, biting, screaming, and yelling, all the while knowing that this is part of their child's developmental process.

In our judgment, children who are having a particularly difficult time managing their aggressive impulses are easily over-stimulated by violent toys. When such children are given toy guns, handcuffs, knives, swords, and masks, they are often lured into the very behavior that they need help to contain and control. We also believe that violent video games are damaging to a child's burgeoning impulse control. This is not the age for sending mixed messages. Do we really need to teach a two-year-old that it is good to shoot, stomp, kick, and try to kill aliens on the screen of a toy, while at the same time giving them a time-out for biting their brother at the park? Imagine the subtle confusion experienced by the child who is rewarded in a game many times for the very behavior that is punished at home and at preschool.

Most children are trying to become self-sufficient in their daily tasks. Too much isolation in this developmental period means less opportunity to practice social skills and can lead to the belief that it is wrong to be independent. If your child craves social interaction, even the slickest high-speed graphics can produce only a pale imitation of a real, live playmate. Fatigue kicks in for most parents of preschoolers. These little ones are so busy and demand so much attention from us it is easy to opt for a break and turn to an electronic gaming toy to occupy the child's time.

So it is an understandable phenomenon that the jacket pockets of many preschoolers bulge with Game Boys and Nintendos. Yet what parents often don't know when they buy these toys is how hard it will be to effectively set limits upon their use. If you are going to give your child a hand-held electronic gaming device, be aware that it is often extremely difficult to avoid power struggles, tantrums, and meltdowns when it becomes time to turn it off. After all, this is the age of power struggles, and, if you add the effects this gaming device has on the pleasure center of your child's brain, you have created a recipe for trouble.

Said Alice, the mother of a three-year-old: "If I only knew how my daughter would react when I turned the game off, I never would have bought the thing!" In agreement, Peter, the father of a four-year-old, told us, "These things should come with a warning label that says, 'Turn off with extreme caution.'"

Technology as a Pacifier

Remember the old adage that "children should be seen and not heard?" Most of us cringe in response. Certainly in our modern culture we want children to express themselves.

It was through the observation of Jessica's behavior that we first began to view Game Boys as the new pacifier of a whole generation of children. They have also become a very common transitional object, replacing the ragged blanket or dog-eared stuffed animal as the toy to have in hand when mom or dad is away. It is not unusual to see a child with a pacifier in the mouth until age three and a hand-held game in their grasp from then on. For those adults who believe that a quiet child is a good child, the use of such electronic devices is clearly a tool for behavioral control. When you also consider the number of children who are taking prescription medications such as Strattera, Ritalin, or Adderall to control impulsive behavior, one cannot help but wonder about the long-term effects on our culture. Perhaps we really *do* want our children to be seen and not heard.

On Amazon.com, a mother of a three-year-old wrote the following review of a product called V.Smile: "I love the fact that he has fun while he's learning his ABCs, colors, and shapes without him even noticing… Before I purchased this item, my son would only play with his Nintendo GameCube or his Sony PlayStation2 and I would feel guilty letting him play because the game systems weren't teaching my son anything. But now I let him play as long as he wants. So trust me, it's worth it!"

Jake

During a recent parenting consultation, a mother shared her frustration with her four-year-old son Jake's obsession with his Game Boy:

> My husband and I were shopping at Wal-Mart and we had our two children with us. The baby was sitting in the front of the shopping cart and Jake was sitting in the back. Jake shouted to me that he wanted to play with his Game Boy, which I had in my purse. I told him no because he had just pulled his sister's hair and made her cry. The next thing I know he has climbed out of the cart and is running down the aisle yelling, "Help. Help. My mommy is trying to kill me!" He ran away from me and my husband, hiding under the clothing racks and screaming at the top of his lungs. We were so embarrassed. The store clerks assisted us, but they looked at me like I was some kind of child abuser.

Another mother told of her latest power struggle with her four-year-old son:

> *We were driving in the van with the whole family. I looked through the rearview mirror and saw my youngest boy going through my bag and trying to find the Game Boy that I had taken away from him earlier that morning. I yelled at him to leave it alone or there would be consequences. He picked it up and threw it at me, hitting me on the back of my head while I was driving. I was so lucky that I didn't get into a traffic accident.*

Whether or not we are willing to admit it, hand-held gaming toys are commonly used for behavioral control. Parenting is an exhausting business and it is very tempting to give in to the Game Boy in exchange for twenty or thirty minutes of uninterrupted time. If this only happened once a week, it would not be a concern. Parents are often overheard complaining about their child's seemingly obsessive behavior. They see the zombie look come over their son's or daughter's face. They observe the tunnel vision, and see the rapidly moving fingers. Yet despite their complaints, our children are spending an average of seven hours a week engaged in gaming activities. This is in addition to the twenty-one hours per week already spent watching TV. In early childhood, it is essential that children learn the ability to control their own impulses and develop the capacity to self-soothe. With a strong dependency on an electronic babysitter, how will they ever learn?

Instant Gratification

Self-soothing contributes to the development of patience and the understanding that others also have needs. Children who can self-soothe are able to use coping skills to calm themselves. According to Dr. Marilyn Benoit, a child and adolescent psychiatrist and a past president of the American Academy of Child and Adolescent Psychiatry,

> *Impatient children suffer more than just meltdowns. When they haven't been taught or given the opportunity to delay their own gratification, children have a harder time empathizing with others and even coping when life becomes challenging... Impatience is hardly unusual or even abnormal in a two-year-old, but meltdown-level impatience in older children can be a sign of more serious problems.*

Decreased frustration tolerance, which is the high price of indulgence, has contributed to a disturbing trend of rages and outbursts among seven- to ten-year-olds. If you are the parent of a preschooler, the time to focus on the development of patience and delayed gratification is *now*. Ask yourself the following questions:

o   Do I believe that children should always be entertained?

o   Do I believe that I must meet all of my child's needs as soon as they arise?

o   Do I believe that it is bad to be made to wait?

o   Do I feel guilty if my child is unhappy?

A recent television commercial advertises a new minivan. In the first scene, a family is shown driving on a picturesque desert highway. The parents are sitting in the front seats smiling and looking through the rear view mirror at the three children seated behind them. The children are shown engaged with their own personal technology. The two children on the outside seats are staring ahead at their own private screens, likely watching movies. The middle child, who does not have his own screen, stares at his hand-held computer game. A voice-over announces the tag line: "The way family car rides were meant to be."

We live in a hurried society, one in which fast food is handy and family meals are disappearing. Families often rush from one activity to the next. No one wants to waste precious time waiting. We want things to be available when we need them. Popular culture has evolved to resemble the two-year-old who demands, "I want a cookie NOW!" Computer gaming fits neatly into our fast-paced society with its instant rewards and immediate entertainment.

As parents, we have the ability to create home environments that don't reflect the hectic pace of the outside world. We have the ability to create a haven for our children, in an environment that teaches tolerance and patience. Our homes can be the place where family members come together to model compassion and cooperation. A place where it is OK to sit with your own thoughts and wait, if need be, for others. A safe home where tolerating a bit of unhappiness can lead to the development of personal responsibility. Where children can learn from their mistakes and have the opportunity to develop their own individual identity.

It is the judgment of the authors that there is no psychological benefit to introducing screen on technology too early. It is also our belief it is only through being *seen and heard* that children can learn to interact effectively with others. And good social skill development is one of the strongest predictors of high self-esteem.

Cyber Dick and Cyber Jane

As we discussed earlier, children's knowledge about sex, gender, and gender-role expectations develops quite early (usually before age three). Preschool children are in the process of finding their gender identity, trying to understand what distinguishes girls from boys. Often they will gravitate toward traditional stereotypes in trying on gender roles at this age.

Little boys may pretend to be firefighters, police officers, cowboys, or soldiers. Little girls may pretend to be a mother, nurse, princess, or schoolteacher. Many parents have some strong beliefs about the role of gender stereotypes in our culture. If you want to encourage flexibility in your child's perception of what it is to be male or female, be sure to provide a variety of books, games, dress-up clothes, and toys that can act to balance some of the stereotypical models that concern you.

We strongly advise against allowing preschool children to play video games. However, if your child *is* playing video or computer games, be sure you notice the manner in which males and females are depicted. If you want to encourage your daughter to identify herself outside of the stereotypical role, then point her toward the few games in existence that feature strong, competent girls and women engaging in important and exciting things — flying airplanes, navigating ships, saving lives, creating art, curing diseases. However, this may be difficult. According to the research organization Children Now, only 16 percent of gaming characters are female and half of those are not active participants — they are merely props or bystanders. If you want to encourage your son to identify himself outside of the traditional male stereotype, then steer him to those games that depict boys and men engaging in exciting team activities that require the skills of cooperation, listening, and problem-solving in a non-violent manner.

Computer software that is designed for preschoolers often includes lead characters that are depicted as animals. Software designed for this age group does a much better job overall compared to those in all other age groups when it comes to offering a variety of roles to both boys and girls. And because the main character is a purple dinosaur or a red dog, there is less racial stereotyping. Yet even with Dora the Explorer and Carmen Sandiego, lead characters, whether human or animal, are typically male and the voice is generally that of a Caucasian. Be aware that some of the most popular preschool gaming software will be introducing sex role stereotypes to your child.

Especially for Parents of Boys

As much as we may try to raise our children with no gender bias, we all know that there are some basic differences between boys and girls. Generally it is our sons who have more difficulty letting go of their electronic games. They seem to get more caught up in obsessive gaming behavior and can be drawn to graphic violence. Here are a few tips to help boys stay grounded while playing electronic games (adapted from an article in the *Lewis and Clark Chronicle*):

o Be aware of the effect of cultural influences. Teach your son that there are many ways to be a male in our society, that there are ways to resolve conflict other than the violent ways that are predominant in games. Praise their efforts to use non-aggressive methods to resolve their problems.

o Use indirect approaches. It is easiest for boys to express their more vulnerable feelings in an indirect manner. Have him participate in an activity (playing tetherball, shooting baskets, walking the dog), and then ask him how a character in a movie or game might have felt in a given situation.

o Build his interpersonal skills. We know that young boys often pay more attention to objects like cars and computers than faces, emotions, and relationships. This can lead to problems relating to people. Coach them to make eye contact with adults and their peers, to give and receive a compliment, and to understand another's feelings.

o Teach regulation. Yes, boys tend to have more physical energy than girls. Teach them that there are appropriate ways to be physically aggressive and provide those outlets. But along with this they will also need to learn how to put the brakes on these aggressive impulses. The games "red light/green light" and "Simon says" incorporate both activity and awareness and can help young children with regulation.

Video Game Marketing to Preschoolers

Often the packaging of video games contains glowing promises of how it will improve your child's life. They often quote software reviewers who are paid to promote game sales. Advertisers have begun to move away from trying to market to you, the parent, and focus on directly selling to your child. Consider that these popular games all have cute main characters, each with their own toy line.

o   Dora the Explorer
o   Barney
o   Carmen Sandiego — Junior Detective
o   Freddy Fish
o   Clifford
o   Little Bill
o   Curious George

The American Academy of Pediatrics recommends limiting video game and computer game use. Total screen time, which includes both television and computer use, should be limited to one to two hours daily. They recommend that children younger than five years should play with computer or video games only if they are developmentally appropriate and accompanied by a parent or caretaker. In addition, no screen time should be allowed prior to the age of three.

What Parents Can Do

o   Give your child many opportunities to socialize with other children.
o   Don't avoid playgroups if your child behaves poorly. Use these as teaching points and keep giving your child the opportunity to be successful with his or her peers.
o   Do not take tantrums personally. You have not failed. Your child is engaged in testing limits, just as most do at this age. Expect to

have your decisions challenged. Be prepared with the tools to set those limits and maintain consistency.

o   Take a Love & Logic parenting course.

o   Teach your child to soothe herself. When your child is upset, don't try to solve the problem yourself. Engage them in the process. Ask questions such as, "What can you do to feel better right now?" "How can mommy or daddy help you?"

o   Introduce television gradually. Be present and watch with your child. Select videos or DVDs that you have previewed to avoid the advertisements on commercial television. Start the healthy habit of participating and protecting your child's use of electronic entertainment.

o   Do not allow your child to eat meals while sitting in front of the TV.

o   Do not allow a television or computer in your child's bedroom.

o   Wait until age seven or eight to introduce handheld computer games and console gaming systems (Game Boy, Nintendo, PlayStation, and XBox).

o   Limit total screen time to fewer than two hours a day.

6
Elementary School Years

Eight- to eighteen-year-olds in the United States spend, on average, almost six and a half hours consuming media in a typical day. Considering that they often use more than one medium at a time, youth of that age actually consume an average of eight and a half hours of media a day, according to the Kaiser Foundation (2005).

Net Geners and *Generation Y* are labels used to denote the generation of children who were born into a computerized world. Many wonder what type of influence this immersion in technology will ultimately have on their lives. As counselors, we encourage families to view technology as a tool and we help them help their children develop well-rounded lives. Parents need to set the example and teach responsible use of such potentially addictive technology. Will our children become savvy users of technology or will the technology itself end up defining them?

Your Child and Stress

The majority of elementary school referrals that come to our counseling offices involve six- to eight-year-olds with anger management problems. The transition to kindergarten is a critical period. Children struggle to gain academic competence, as school is the important event at this stage. They learn to make things, use tools, and acquire new skills — all while transitioning from the world of *home* into the world of *peers*. And in this new world are many rules a child must master.

Some rules are explicit and are taught by the teacher (lining-up at recess time or raising your hand when you have a question). Other, less obvious, rules include the ability to read the subtle cues of body language and non-verbal communication. Such skills help children navigate through new situations with less difficulty. Childhood is so complex, challenging, and frustrating that it's no wonder many kids display anger problems during this period.

In this chapter we will explore our four primary concerns about elementary and middle school age children who game intensively:

1. Delayed emotional development
2. Impaired social skills
3. Bullying and victimization
4. Obesity

We will also explore the effects of gaming on the children who are most vulnerable to developing addictions — those who have attention deficit disorder and those who struggle with excessive shyness. We will also consider the social needs of school-age children, discuss the disappearance of recess, and offer guidance to parents.

As counselors involved in determining a child's readiness for school, we are saddened and concerned that the current emphasis on children's academic preparedness continues to overshadow social and emotional development. Children can learn to regulate their emotions in pro-social or anti-social ways. The way they behave will greatly influence their ability to respond to peer pressure. In elementary school, peer relationships begin to take center stage.

Children who have desirable social skills, are willing to share, and are friendly and patient have the easiest time adjusting. Their social confidence gives them a sense of competence that, in turn, eases their academic adjustment to the new learning environment. Children between the ages of eight and eighteen who read more and play fewer video games are more likely to get better grades in school (Kaiser Family Foundation, 2005).

As soon as they enter into a school environment, children begin to form tightly knit inner circles, creating their own group identity by looking and talking alike, perhaps creating a secret handshake, and believing that they are "cooler" than those on the outside looking in. It is common for kids to feel a strong pressure to dress and speak in a particular way, or wear their hair in a specific style. They may decide that Mondays are "dress in pink days," or that Friday means "bring your Pokemon cards." These inner circles provide positive support systems where children feel secure with one another.

These newly formed peer relationships can also be the source of much stress. Children can be mean and judgmental, and can quickly label others. Even if your child doesn't act in this manner, he may feel pressure to share the beliefs of his friends because he is concerned about what his friends think of him. While it may seem harsh, it's worth remembering that your child is getting an advanced lesson in social skill development. This challenge offers the opportunity for him to try out what he has learned at home on a larger stage.

This is also a time when children *really* want to play video games. The majority of second- and third-graders report that they play computer games and can usually tell you about their favorite. Playing XBox at a friend's house and saving up allowance to buy a popular new game are among the favorite activities of this age group. Their holiday wish lists will likely contain a few software titles. If you allow your grade school-aged child to engage in gaming, here are four important questions to ask yourself:

1. Can my child maintain friendships?
2. Do his peers accept him?
3. How does he handle anger?
4. Does he get enough exercise?

Your answers to these questions can also guide you in selecting appropriate time limits for their gaming activities as well as the content of the games that they will play. Take a more conservative and cautious approach to gaming if your child has difficulty with peer relationships or is not getting enough exercise. If there has been a problem with aggressive behavior, don't allow your child to play first-person shooter games.

Delayed Emotional Development

First and second grade is also the time when the symptoms of attention deficit hyperactivity disorder (ADHD) are most likely to surface. The following case involves Jonathan, a first grader with anger problems and symptoms of ADHD. His parents introduced computer games at an early age and were very reluctant to place any limitations on his use.

Jonathan

Six-year-old Jonathan was an active child who had a strong drive to be busy. He was petite with short blond hair and usually came home from school covered in dirt. Jonathan was very physical by nature and was happiest when climbing or jumping. He talked a lot, often too loud. He interrupted and had trouble listening to others. His peers at school said that he didn't share well, and they didn't like to play with him. Teachers were concerned because his outbursts were disruptive to the class. Jonathan's mother felt sad that her son was being picked on by the other children.

The youngest of the family, Jonathan had three older siblings who often played violent, first-person shooter games when Jonathan was a baby. Thus, Jonathan began playing violent video games as a toddler. As soon as he could walk, he was reaching for the joystick. His siblings picked on him and they often fought over use of their gaming console.

Exhausted, his mother Carol brought him in for counseling because she was worried that if his behaviors did not change, Jonathan would always be an outsider.

His father George was not concerned. He regarded as a success his son's ability to focus for hours when playing computer games. "If you need him to cooperate, use gaming terms," George told us. "He and I spend hours playing Halo together. We have a special language that we understand. When you use the right words he will listen. I have no problem getting him to sit still. The teachers just don't care enough to learn to relate to him at his advanced level. They should use video game time as a reward in the classroom."

At the conclusion of Jonathan's evaluation, his parents were given several recommendations designed to help with their son's adjustment to grade school. They were advised to have him tested for learning disabilities and ADD. Additionally, it was strongly recommended that the video game console be removed from the home, and that his parents incorporate other activities into their individual time with their son. They were told that Jonathan was not very good at interpreting social cues, and therefore would need individual time with his parents to focus on social skills. They were given a list of suggested activities that would encourage his development.

Of all of recommendations that they received, the one that they could not agree with was removal of the gaming console. "I don't want to take the games away from him; they are the only things that make him happy," said Carol. "You mean that they are the only things that make him sit still while you are making dinner," interrupted her husband. "And what about our other children? Should they be punished because their brother has problems?"

We don't view removing video games as a punishment. After all a game is just a game, isn't it? Based on our experience, the following activities are recommended for children with ADD:

o   Spend fifteen minutes of individual time each day with each parent to help your child focus. These exercises can be playful.

o   Take a walk and play "red light/green light" along the way.

o   Cook while following a recipe.

o   Read out loud.

o   Play "Simon says."

o   Learn to play a musical instrument.

Impaired Social Skills

Beginning at a very young age, shyness is one of the most easily recognized traits in children. Shyness will affect the child's adaptability in many situations at school. It's important for parents to demonstrate their acceptance of the child and to encourage her self-esteem. Since it is primarily new situations and new people that evoke the withdrawal response, the shy child will usually adapt with time, familiarity, and acceptance.

A big concern is the development of social skills. You can help your child develop these by providing the opportunity for her to interact with a familiar group of children over a long period of time. Since the class-room composition changes each year, you can help her maintain long-term friendships in the neighborhood, church, and community.

For some middle-years children, social situations and interactions can be terrifying. When they come in contact with new children, they rarely feel at ease. Typically, they are unwilling or unable to make the first move, preferring to abandon a potential friendship rather than reach out to the unfamiliar. A few of these timid children may be emotionally distressed, but they are in the minority. In fact, some children are just naturally withdrawn and slow to warm up in new situations.

From our experiences, we notice that introverted children easily get absorbed into computer games. Perhaps it is the easiest access to social situations that don't require much participation on their part. Or, perhaps it's the fact that they can stay in their comfort zone (home) while talking to others.

Ian

Eleven-year-old Ian was a sixth grader who never felt like he fit in with his friends at school. His mother, Diane, brought him in for counseling after she overheard him having a violent conversation with another player while playing SoCom's Navy Seals, a console game that connects players to one another through the Internet. They can also use a microphone to communicate directly. One afternoon when she got home early from work, she heard her son shouting obscenities: "Die you mother, I'll kill you quickly." "Ha ha, you suck!" "Take that you faggot!" She could hear the voices of the other players screaming their own obscenities. Some voices sounded like they came from boys her son's age, but some were those of adult men! She had never heard her son speak that way before. "And what are adult men doing playing video games at three in the afternoon in the middle of the work week?" she wondered.

Three in the afternoon in the state of Washington is actually 11 PM in Algeria, 8 PM in Brazil, and 7 AM in South Korea. Diane had not considered that her son would be exposed to all kinds of players from all over the world. She didn't know that the average gamer is a thirty-three-year-old male. Neither was she prepared for her son to be exposed to uncensored swearing, racism, sexism, and homophobia.

Ian had always been a shy child. He didn't like new situations and always liked to stay close to home. "Getting him to go to a birthday party was like pulling teeth!" she admitted. So she was pleased that he wanted to become more interactive on-line.

Ian's story has a happy ending. A bright, sensitive boy, he did well in his counseling sessions. After some time he came to know more about his own nature. He learned that he was introverted and what this meant. He absorbed suggestions from a book called *The Introvert Advantage* that described how an introvert could be more comfortable in an extroverted world. Soon he talked about wanting to be comfortable with his peers at school and wanting close friends. Diane actively participated in Ian's counseling. A natural extrovert, Diane needed to learn about how to be more effective in parenting her introverted child. She learned how to help Ian be more comfortable in social situations. Together it was decided that he didn't need to stop gaming completely. Instead, limits were agreed on.

Five years later we checked in with Ian and Diane. What we heard was very positive; he was doing well in high school and had recently asked a girl to go to Homecoming with him. "She said yes — it was soooo cool," he shared with pride. His home life seemed quite normal. He was still playing Navy Seals, but only when he didn't have something better to do. "Yeah, I love that game," he admitted, "but it's no big deal anymore."

Bullying and Victimization

Maggie, a former patient of ours, was a pretty eight-year-old girl of Filipino descent. She was petite and friendly. Most adults perceived her to be sweet and kind. She always had a smile and was very compliant with adults.

Maggie was also a bully. She was suspended from school for sending an inappropriate message to a classmate via the school e-mail system. Her third grade class had just been trained to use the Internet and each student was assigned an e-mail address. One day while playing at recess, she approached a girl named Tiffany at the playground and asked her to play. She said no. Maggie asked her why not, and the girl told her it was because she just wanted to play by herself. Later that afternoon when Maggie got home, she wrote an e-mail to Tiffany telling her that she was a "fat pig." Maggie also copied this to all of her classmates. The next morning, Maggie was sent to the principal's office, her parents were called in, and she was suspended.

Maggie's parents brought her in for counseling. They were mortified and couldn't believe that their little girl could be that cruel. Through counseling she learned that her actions have consequences. She didn't realize that she could cause so much pain merely with the click of a mouse. She never would have called Tiffany a name to her face. But with the anonymity of the computer, she could, and did.

In recent years there has been a rise in bullying behavior perpetrated by girls. This may be linked to the fact that kids are more engaged in solitary game play and, as a result, lack important peer group interaction skills. Girls also may be conditioned to express their aggression is non-direct ways. Maggie needed to learn healthy ways to express her anger. Like many children her age, she lacked the ability to be assertive with her peers at school.

While gaming wasn't the source of her problem, her story demonstrates why school-age children should not play on-line computer or console games. In on-line role-playing games, there is another layer of distance between players. Character names, with anonymity, can lead to intense, verbally abusive behavior by some players. In the fantasy game world there are few consequences for such behavior. And since players don't know one another, there is a lack of accountability. Kids know that other players are not going to call their parents and tell on them.

Evan Ramsey

Have you noticed the sign posted on the grounds of elementary schools? The one that reads, "Gun-Free Zone?"

This sign didn't seem to faze Evan Ramsey who on February 9, 1997, shot and killed two people and wounded two others in a shooting at Bethel High School in Bethel, Alaska. Ramsey was a sophomore at the time. We mention him here because like many children who go on to commit murder, he was repeatedly bullied at school. Elementary school is typically where such behavior begins. He also played violent video games.

According to two studies appearing in the American Psychological Association's *2000 Journal of Personality and Social Psychology,* playing violent video games like Doom, Wolfenstein, or Mortal Kombat can increase a person's aggressive thoughts, feelings, and behaviors both in laboratory settings and in actual life. The three games happen to be popular among kids in grades four, five, and six. Fifty-nine percent of fourth grade girls and 73 percent of fourth grade boys say that the majority of their favorite video games are violent (Anderson, 2001).

Evan Ramsey was reportedly picked on frequently at school. According to friends, he wasn't very smart and was often called such names as "retard," "spaz," or "braindead." The experts say educators should learn a key lesson from the more than two dozen school shootings since the killings at Columbine High School in 1999 because troubled teens who plan attacks often warn of their intentions. Parents complain that schools are not doing enough to recognize and report potential threatening behaviors. Most parents agree that every school should have a plan of action to prevent bullying. Many such plans include metal detectors.

The authors want all parents to remember that *they* have the power to make a much greater impact on their children than schools ever will. If your child is having social problems, you can pull the plug on violent video games. By doing so, you may not completely solve this problem. But you will take away one contributing factor and replace it with a potent antidote — *parental involvement.*

The authors believe that violent video games may be more harmful for bullied children than violent television and movies. Why? Because such games are interactive, very engrossing, and require the player to identify with the aggressor. And while it may be empowering for a bullied child to shoot at the bad guys in a game, this action will not improve their personal problems. The way to combat bullying is to teach a child *assertiveness* in the real world with people they know, a difficult skill to master at any age.

The Obesity Epidemic

The annual National Health and Nutrition Examination Survey conducted by the Centers for Disease Control and Prevention found that about one-third of all American children — twenty-five million — are overweight.

Approximately 30.3 percent of children (aged six to eleven) are overweight and 15.3 percent are obese. For teens twelve to nineteen, the rate is almost identical: 33.4 percent overweight and 15.5 percent obese (American Obesity Association, 2006).

Video games cannot be held solely responsible for the epidemic of childhood obesity. We do, however, think that any childhood sedentary activity that has an addictive quality (such as gaming) should be considered as a contributing factor. Children, aged eight to eighteen, spend more time (over forty-four hours per week) in front of computer, television, and game screens than any other activity in their lives except sleeping (Kaiser Family Foundation, 2005).

Of course, there are many other factors that contribute to this epidemic including the disappearance of physical education (PE) curriculum in our schools, the large number of children who are home alone after school, our love of fast food, poor sleep habits, and overly scheduled lifestyles.

A recent study showed a relationship between playing video games and obesity. Researchers at the University of Texas at Austin surveyed almost three thousand children from one to twelve years old, recording their habits, and calculating body mass indices. They found that the children who played video games were more likely to be overweight than children who watched television and didn't play video games.

But there is a twist. This study concluded that playing video games *could be a result* of obesity, rather than the other way around. The researchers theorized that because overweight children are more sedentary and have fewer friends, they may simply find themselves with more free time on their hands that they fill with video games.

The Surgeon General of the United States offers the following recommendations to prevent obesity:

o   Be physically active. It is recommended that Americans accumulate at least thirty minutes (adults) or an hour (children) of moderate physical activity most days of the week. Even greater amounts of physical activity may be necessary for the prevention of weight gain, for weight loss, or for sustaining weight loss.

o   Plan family activities that provide everyone with exercise and enjoyment.

o   Provide a safe environment for your children and their friends to play actively; encourage swimming, biking, skating, ball sports, and other fun activities.

o   Reduce the amount of time you and your family spend in sedentary activities such as watching TV or playing video games. Limit screen time to fewer than two hours a day.

What Parents Can Do

o   Stay connected. The media bombard our children with information about pop culture every day. Let your home be a haven for your child. A place where ideas are exchanged and he or she is loved for who they are, not how they look or what they wear. A child should always fit in at home!

o   Ensure that your child develops healthy social skills. If your child is home schooled or has limited exposure to peer groups, be cautious about the amount of time that is allotted for gaming.

o   Have regular conversations about bullying and peer pressure. Do they know someone who is bullied? Have they ever felt picked on? Which child in their classroom gets picked on the most?

o   If your child has an anger management problem, do not allow him to play violent video games. No exceptions!

o   No on-line games until age fourteen, unless you are going to play on-line with your child.

o   Limit screen time to two to three hours per day. This excludes computer time that is necessary for homework. Remember to consider total screen time (TV, iPod, computer, etc.).

o   No Internet in your child's bedroom.

o   Are you in charge at home? As children become preteens, it is essential to maintain an authoritative role in your home. Be willing to be unpopular if necessary — disconnect the Internet, unplug the mouse, remove the console, and throw away the game.

7
Adolescence

In the past we thought of the brain as being fully developed by adolescence. Recent research has proven this wrong. With the advent of specialized technologies like the MRI, scientists have now discovered that brain growth continues well into the third decade of life. The major changes that occur during adolescence primarily involve the frontal cortex — a part of the brain that has been referred to as its "CEO" and is located just behind the forehead. The frontal cortex has a wide range of functions including the processing and organizing of information, controlling our ability to plan effectively, and remembering with accuracy. It also plays a role in modulating our moods.

During the teenage years there is an internal drive towards action and an upheaval in the sense of self. Teens are striving towards *individuation* (an open-ended process of psychological maturity). With so many factors

at work — brain growth, hormonal changes, and psychosocial development — it is no wonder that parents of teenagers pour into counseling
offices all across the nation asking, "Where did my child go?"

Adolescence is a time of impulsivity, intensity, and acting out. It is
also a time of heightened creativity and curiosity about the world. There
are many rewards to parenting your teen. The recipe for success involves
setting and maintaining healthy boundaries while building your
relationship with a respect for your son's or daughter's perspective.

True to their developmental stage, teens are more adventurous and
explore more in Cyberspace. They track down stories that interest them
and venture into some of the Internet's darker corners. Some, through the
veil of perceived anonymity, will become emboldened to take greater
risks. This is why computer or video gaming still needs to be closely
monitored. This is a phase in our children's development that requires us
to be on our toes and be present with our children.

When talking about teens and their gaming habits, we hear so many
parents say, "Well at least he is at home at night!" While we understand
this, we want parents to know that teens don't need to leave your house
to find trouble. Just because your child is physically in your home, don't
be lulled into a false sense of security. Sitting in front of their computers,
they have Cyberspace at their fingertips. On-line they can meet the type
of predator that might never come in contact with them in a real-life
community. With a click of the mouse they can be at risk of:

o   Seeing graphically violent and/or sexual images.
o   Meeting a convicted sex offender.
o   Being harassed or sexually solicited.

As your child ages, the popular computer games will have more
mature content. Games that are rated "T" for teen often contain blood,

gore, sex, and violence. This is also the age when on-line games are in demand and peer pressure brings new challenges.

The five most pressing concerns for teens and gaming are

1. Sleep deprivation: a significant cause of accidents among teen drivers and school absenteeism
2. Dropping out: an inability to stay on the path with their peers
3. Peer pressure: making it more difficult to follow family guide-lines
4. Aggression toward the outside world: identification with violence as means of solving problems
5. Exposure to sexual solicitation: predatory adults frequently play these games and commonly "hit" on other players

Sleep Deprivation

Too much TV or computer games can affect sleep. Many adolescents prefer to be awake until 1 or 2 AM. Most will tell you that their favorite thing to do during the middle of the night is to go on-line and play a game or browse Internet chat rooms. According to studies by the National Sleep Foundation, it is clear that the presence of other media, such as a computer, video games, or Internet in a kid's bedroom is associated with poor sleep.

Adolescents also experience a change in their sleep patterns — their bodies want to stay up late and wake up later, which often leads to catching up on sleep during the weekend. During adolescence, the body's circadian rhythm (sort of like an internal biological clock) is reset, telling a teen to fall asleep later at night and wake up later in the morning. Why? Because *melatonin*, a brain hormone, is produced later at night in teens than it is for kids and adults, making it harder for teens to fall asleep.

This sleep schedule irregularity can actually aggravate the problem and make it harder to sleep at a reasonable hour. Excessive gaming only makes the problem worse.

The National Sleep Foundation's
Guidelines for Children and Adolescents

Age	Nighttime Sleep (hours)	Daytime Sleep (hours)	Total Sleep (hours)
1 month	8.5 (many naps)	7.5 (many naps)	16
3 months	6-10	5-9	15
6 months	10-12	3-4.5	14.5
9 months	11	3 (2 naps)	14
12 months	11	2.5 (2 naps)	13.5
18 months	11	2.5 (1-2 naps)	13.5
2 years	11	2 (1 nap)	13
3 years	10.5	1.5 (1 nap)	12
4 years	11.5	0	11.5
5 years	11	0	11
6 years	11	0	11
7 years	11	0	11
8 years	10-11	0	10-11
9 years	10-11	0	10-11
10 years	10	0	10
11 years	10	0	10
12-13 years	9.5-10	0	9.5-10
14 years	9.5	0	9.5
15 years	9.5	0	9.5
16 years	9.25	0	9.25

Your child doesn't need a shot of adrenaline at 2 AM, nor does she need frontal lobe stimulation late at night. What adolescents *need* (but few get) is about eight to nine and a half hours of sleep per night. And as they progress through puberty, teens actually need more sleep. Because they often have schedules packed with school and activities, typically they are chronically sleep deprived (lacking a healthy amount of sleep). And sleep deprivation adds up over time, so an hour less per night is like a full night without sleep by the end of the week. Among other things, sleep deprivation can lead to:

o   Decreased attentiveness
o   Decreased short-term memory
o   Inconsistent performance
o   Delayed response time
o   Obesity

Poor sleep can also cause temper problems, school problems, high stimulant use (too many highly caffeinated energy drinks), and driving accidents (more than half of "asleep-at-the-wheel" car accidents are caused by teens). Many parents are shocked when they begin to count how many cans of Rock Star and Red Bull "energy drinks" their kids are drinking in any given week.

Dropping Out

Alex, whom we visited in an earlier chapter, was seventeen years old. He was a withdrawn, quiet young man who had trouble making eye contact. He was overweight and his hygiene was poor. He didn't attend high school last year because his parents said that they "just couldn't get him to go." He spent most of his days and nights locked in his room playing

World of Warcraft. He was always tired. Theresa, his mother, had read a recent *Seattle Times* article on gaming addiction and came to us for help.

We learned that Alex was the last child living at home. He had two older siblings who had already moved away. When he was seven years old, his parents divorced. The divorce was especially difficult for his mother who suffered from depression and was struggling to play an active role with her children. Alex primarily lived with his mother and visited his father occasionally on the weekends. She worked for a utility company and left the house before he did each morning. And because she started her days early, she went to bed much earlier than her son.

When he was fifteen years old, Alex discovered the on-line game World of Warcraft (WOW). Within two months of playing, he began to miss school. "First there were a few sick days, and then he would just flat out refuse to go," reported his mother. "I had taken so much time off from work trying to get Alex to school that I was afraid I would be fired."

The more school that Alex missed, the more out of step he felt with his peers. By the time he came into counseling, he was taking several strong psychiatric medications to help him with the severe anxiety he felt whenever he left his bedroom.

The game quickly became a bargaining tool (if you go to school, then you can play as much WOW as you like). However, his parent set the bar so low (she just required him to go to school) that it didn't matter if he did homework or passed his classes. Her bargaining had no effect. There were power struggles over WOW. Sometimes his mother would take away the computer. Sometimes she would yell at him. Sometimes he would yell back. She would threaten to stop paying the game subscription fee of $14.95 per month. He would threaten to hurt her if she did. In response, she told him that she would call the police on him. Both knew that no matter how bad it got, she never would.

Carly

Carly's case offers a different take on the problems associated with gaming addiction and dropping out. Carly's story asks us to consider what happens to a teenager when a *parent* drops out.

Thirteen-year-old Carly, the oldest of four children, was brought in for counseling by her father, Jeff. Recently he and Carly's mother, Tammy, had divorced and he was worried about the effect this was having on his daughter. Lately Carly had been acting depressed at home and recently admitted to experimenting with marijuana.

During our initial meeting, Jeff spoke of gaming addiction and the traumatic end of his marriage. His wife of fourteen years had left him and the children. She had moved into a nearby apartment and was having a long-distance affair with a man she met while gaming on-line. During the divorce proceedings she gave up custody of her children. At the time of our interview, she hadn't asked to see her children in over three months. Carly's mother had completely abandoned her family.

The seeds had been planted three years earlier when Jeff began playing the on-line role-playing game EverQuest. Tammy started complaining that he was spending too much time gaming. She told him that he was ignoring her and the children. Over the next few months they would often fight about the game. Then Jeff had an idea — he would encourage his wife to play EverQuest, too. If she also played, then she might leave him alone and stop complaining. After some convincing, Tammy created her own EverQuest character and began to play along with her husband. Soon she was playing in the mornings after her kids went to school.

Tammy agreed to participate in one counseling session. During her session she described how unhappy and lonely she had been in her marriage, and how attached she had become to the man she met while gaming. While they gamed together, this new man was kind and flirtatious. She fell in love instantly. After a month of playing on-line together, they started talking on the phone. She didn't mind that he lived in Montana; their long distance romance made her happy. A year later she decided to leave her family and pursue a life with her boyfriend. He, however, didn't want this. Despite his refusals to meet with her, she showed up on his doorstep anyway. What Tammy found was a twenty-three-year-old man who was still living at home with his parents in their basement.

During her session, Tammy did not show any concern about her children's welfare. She admitted to playing EverQuest sixty to seventy hours per week. She even asked the counselor to help her learn how to improve her relationship with her young man!

These two stories illustrate what can happen when gamers neglect their real-world lives. In Carly's case there was a type of domino effect where her father's absorption into the world of gaming triggered the detachment of his wife and perhaps the substance abuse of his daughter. The more disconnected we are from friends and family the more vulnerable we are to forming on-line attachments. For Alex, the detachment from his mother due to her depression left him more susceptible to forming Cyberspace attachments and less capable of living in the real world. There is no doubt that families need nurturing, but with today's technologies, family members who are feeling neglected can easily find comfort with someone on-line.

Peer Pressure Cyber-style

One might think that on-line peer pressure would be easier to resist than that in real life. It is surprising how easy it is to become enmeshed in on-line communities.

In the world of on-line gaming, many goals are required in order to advance or *level up*. Each new level offers its own rewards: money (gold/silver), greater abilities, better armor and equipment, and specialized skills. In order to *level up*, your character needs to complete specific tasks. Characters are divided into a variety of classes, each with their own distinct abilities. Warrior, shaman, guardian, wizard, necromancer, captain, druid, hunter, and priest are examples of the types of classes from which a player may choose. Many tasks cannot be completed by a single player; they require a joint effort with other players. The higher your character's level, the higher the number of players you will need. Killing a beast may require the combined talents of a priest, captain, wizard, and shaman.

Guilds and *fellowships* are formed. They can evolve into highly exclusive cliques in which players exert a strong influence upon one another. Often they have a hierarchical structure with a guild leader and officers. These leaders actively recruit new members. Some guilds have a military structure; others resemble a fraternity. Many guilds have their own Websites. Along with membership comes an expectation of loyalty and commitment. Teams are organized and come together to complete quests. Agreements are made and appointments are set. Imagine an army regiment, with front-line infantry, specialized forces, medics, and communication specialists all coming together to complete a mission. If your son's character is his group's designated *medic* (healer), then he had best show up, or, well…you get the picture.

This creates a whole new form of peer pressure. If you are paying a monthly subscription fee so that your teen can participate in on-line gaming, then we strongly advise you to do some research. Do an Internet search by the game's name and visit the Websites that are listed. Read some of the comments (postings) and follow the threads to learn more about the culture and guilds associated with the game. It is apparent that for some players, their on-line world has become a substitute for real-life *community*.

Aggression

The United States Army knows the power of computer games. They routinely use games that they call "multipurpose arcade combat simulators" to help prepare soldiers to respond successfully on the battlefield. These games offer a soldier the opportunity to practice for combat situations in a simulated environment that desensitizes him to the violence he will discover on the battlefield. Thus, it's easier for him to pull the trigger and respond without hesitation to life or death situations. These training games are similar to commercially available, first-person shooter games. Apparently, the U.S. military knows that teens are drawn to playing violent video games and is capitalizing on this by teaming up with commercial companies to create recruitment games. An example of this is a free game called "America's Army." It is a tactical game designed to boost enlistment and encourage young people to explore a career in the military.

Many of the video and computer games that are most popular with our teens center on the act of killing. It may be the killing of other players in an on-line role-playing game (RPG) in a simulated combat zone (Battlefield, Navy Seals), or the killing of non-player characters

(NPCs) in a console game. The killing may be of fantasy creatures like zombies, aliens, wizards, and ogres or historical military figures such as Hitler or Mussolini. The setting might be in the streets of a ghetto, a fairy-tale castle, or the underworld. Regardless of the location, if the main activity is killing, then learning how to kill, at least electronically, is important to successful game play. This requires a mastery of weaponry and ammunition.

Most gamers know the difference between a halberd, a cutlass, an epee, a claymore, and a broad sword. These same players will also know when it is more effective to use an AK-47, as opposed to an Uzi or an M-16. Along with this they will know how much and what type of ammunition is required to complete their mission. More advanced gamers will learn all of the dimensions of any given weapon right down to its weight and how many rounds it uses per minute. Electronic message boards often feature debates among players if a weapon is not accurately depicted within a game. In a combat situation, a player may also have at his disposal a variety of magic spells and potions along with grenades, tear gas, poison darts, bombs, and daggers.

An avid gamer can also learn the most efficient way to commit a robbery. A very popular character role in many games is that of a *thief*. Success as a thief means knowing how to pick a pocket, case a building, or stab someone in the back. Thieves can be stealthy or overtly violent armed robbers. Think of the popular saying "get rich or die trying" and you get the point. Moreover, in some games your child can get points for shooting prostitutes and drug dealers as well as law enforcement officers! Success in these types of games will often involve mastering various antisocial behaviors.

Whether or not the playing of violent video and computer games leads to the development of aggressive and antisocial behavior has been a subject of controversy since the beginning of gaming. For every study that we could share with you that proves a connection, you can find another that challenges that same conclusion. We do know, however, about the so-called "DC sniper." At seventeen, John Lee Malvo reportedly prepared for his murderous attacks by playing Halo, an XBox shooter game that was played in "sniper mode." However we won't debate the issue here. Instead, we will offer you our professional opinion that does match those of the U.S. Senate Committee on Commerce, Science, & Transportation, and also concurs with the recommendations of the American Medical Association, The American Pediatric Association, the Surgeon General of the United States, The American Psychiatric Association, and the National Mental Health Association:

It is our professional opinion that for some children and teens, high levels of violent video game exposure can result in increased antisocial behavior. The interactive nature of these violent games makes them even more hazardous than other types of media. Immersion into the Cyber world of an ultra violent game has a direct effect on brain functioning and can lead to obsession, addiction, and even to a detachment from reality. We know that not all kids who play such games will become aggressive. We also know from real-life tragedies that a surprisingly high number of young people who become murderers and killers play ultra violent video games.

Here is an excerpt from a recent interview between CNN anchorman Anderson Cooper and Evan Ramsey, the aforementioned murderer (Chapter 6) who killed two and wounded two in a shooting at Bethel High School in Bethel, Alaska:

COOPER: *Over nine years ago, in February 1997, sixteen-year-old Evan Ramsey entered his high school in Bethel, Alaska. He pulled out a twelve-gauge shotgun and murdered a student and the principal. Today he's serving a prison sentence of 198 years at the [Arizona State Prison Complex — Florence.]*

RAMSEY: *There was a list of people that I wanted to shoot at. Keep in mind that I didn't understand how life worked at the time. I didn't know that when you shoot somebody, they don't get back up.*

COOPER: *What do you mean?*

RAMSEY: *I did not understand that if I pull out a gun and shoot you, there's a good chance that you're not getting back up. You're going to bleed to death and die either right there or on the way to the hospital. That part of reality didn't click for whatever reason.*

COOPER: *I think it's probably hard for some people to believe that you didn't know that dead is dead.*

RAMSEY: *I based a lot of my knowledge solely on video games. You shoot a guy in [the video game] Doom and he gets back up. You've got to shoot things in Doom eight or nine times before it dies. And I took that concept from the video game and added it to life. A lot of people can see it as a copout, but they don't stop and think about it. Well, I was sixteen at the time, and although a sixteen-year-old is supposed to know right from wrong, I didn't know it completely.*

COOPER: *What did it feel like to pull the trigger?*

RAMSEY: *I'm going to get what I want. I'm going to scare these people away. Nobody's going to pick on me. There won't be any more verbal or physical abuse from anybody.*

COOPER: *So it felt like relief?*

RAMSEY: *Yes. There was great relief.*

COOPER: *What do you want people to know?*

RAMSEY: *What some kids go through. It's not all that bad. I saw my treatment as the end of everything. If I would have had somebody to sit down with and say, it's not that bad, you don't have to react this way, there's other means, I could have gotten help. It can always be worse, and it can always get better.*

Regardless of whether a direct causal relationship exists or not, it is up to us as parents to ask ourselves: How much exposure to weaponry and killing is healthy for my child? Can long-term exposure to such material have an adverse effect on my teenager? The authors believe that common sense will supply the answer, and we encourage all parents to recognize and respect the risks associated with violent video game play.

Sexual Solicitation

Sexual solicitation is a routine part of many on-line games. There are many adults playing games such as EverQuest, World of Warcraft, Lord of the Rings, City of Heroes, Guild Wars, Final Fantasy, Call of Duty, Company of Heroes, and Halo 3. Most of these players are respectful. However, many are not. The game designers (mostly men) determine the physical components; the player selects from the available options to build their game character. Many female characters have exaggerated physical features that highlight large breasts, long legs, and flowing hair — imagine a Barbie doll in a dominatrix costume with sword and whip.

Make your child aware that they can *never* know who these other players really are by talking with them on-line. They may seem nice, they may offer gifts of high-level loot and armor, they may even rescue you from a dragon — but they are still *strangers*. In the world of on-line gaming, men play female characters, women play male characters, and the people playing them commonly lie about their identities.

Erica

The fact that she could create such a sexualized character is one reason why fourteen-year-old Erica was drawn to play EverQuest. When she was in grade school she spent hours watching her brother play "Duke Nukem," a hand-held shooter game. "I liked watching the pretty girls dancing around the poles," she told her counselor. "My brother and his buds would whistle at them."

She created a seductive female character that was a powerful wizard, her on-line alter ego. She spent hours building up this character and became a much sought after group player. At school she would brag to her girlfriends about all of the men who would flirt with her. She clearly loved being the center of all of this male attention. There was one character she chatted with more than others. Their flirtation built to the point where they exchanged cell phone numbers. Now she was getting his texts, some of which were quite explicit. These she proudly showed her friends.

She learned that he was twenty years old and lived about four hours away from her hometown. One day they made arrangements to meet at the mall and Erica ditched school. They began a secret relationship. Erica loved the attention that he would lavish on her, and he would always buy her something. Soon their meetings took place in a hotel room.

When Erica came into counseling she was four months pregnant; the baby's father had a restraining order against him and he faced rape charges. As extreme as her case may seem, we know that she was one of the lucky ones.

The National Center for Missing and Exploited Children (NCMEC) offers a variety of resources for teens and their parents. We recommend that you and your child visit their Website together. There you will learn what to do in the case of an unwanted solicitation, how to protect your child from a sexual solicitation, and reporting procedures. They also provide a link to a very informative publication entitled, *On-line Victimization: Five Years Later.*

What Parents Can Do

o Maintain a curfew and encourage your child to get enough sleep. Again, be willing to disconnect the Internet at night to enforce your boundary. Take away the car keys if he or she has been gaming all night.

o If your teen engages in on-line gaming, do not allow the Internet in the bedroom. If later they prove to be responsible, older teens can be eased into having more responsibility by being allowed to have the Internet in their rooms. Stay involved. Update their firewalls and check in frequently about their on-line activities.

o If you or your partner plays computer games, it is essential that *you* practice responsible gaming. Your children are watching!

o Teens who are already displaying antisocial behavior (delinquency, angry outbursts, truancy, theft, etc.) should not be allowed to play violent video games under any circumstances.

o Do not allow teens who have had problems with other addictions (alcohol or other drugs) to play on-line games.

And there's one more thing you can do. You can help dispel the mystique about a *career* in the computer gaming field. It has been our experience that many professionals in the gaming industry are highly unsatisfied with their lives. So if your child's greatest desire in life is to develop games, we strongly encourage you to set up a meeting between your child and an actual game developer. During the interview, ask about quality of life issues — how many hours do you work each day, do you like your job, can you have input into the way a game is made, what is a typical workday like, are you married, and do you have children? This exercise will offer your child a realistic peek into this often overly glorified profession.

8
Adult Children Addicted to Gaming

As mentioned earlier in this book, any addiction tends to arrest normal psychological development. Across the country, we are seeing increasing numbers of adult children living at home. They are doing this not because they are in college or because they are working and saving money. They are gaming addicts who either never left home or have returned home. They have dropped out of high school or out of college. They have been fired from their jobs or have never held a job. These young adults feel strong guilt and shame. Their self-esteem is fragile. Because the addiction has them in its grip, their efforts to change are often futile.

Parents of these adults are often at a loss to know how to respond effectively. Their feelings for their children are usually a mix of love, concern, resentment, guilt, shame, puzzlement, and desperation. They wonder what they did wrong while, at the same time, they judge their children as morally flawed, lazy, or weak-willed.

What most of these parents do not understand is that their children are addicted and desperately need help. As with all addictions, however, the family may, in the end, discover that they are powerless to help.

In this section we will offer guidance to parents who find themselves trying to help their adult children who are gaming addicts.

Ben

Ben was twenty-three when his father contacted our office. Ben was addicted to gaming and computer chat rooms. He had dropped out of high school and his family had asked him to leave the home when he turned eighteen. When Ben first moved out, he lived with other gamers that he knew. There, he gamed and lived off his friends until they kicked him out. He then begged his grandparents to take him in. They agreed, but only under certain conditions (help at home, go to school, go to work).

His gaming continued to be the only thing he would focus on and soon his grandparents had had enough. When they turned him out, Ben contacted his father and stepmother once again, begging to return and agreeing to anything his father demanded. His father consented and designed what he called "Daddy Boot Camp." Ben was supposed to adhere to a strict schedule, do specific chores in lieu of paying rent, and go to the local community college to complete his high school credits. Most important, Ben was supposed to limit his computer time to only a few hours per day. Ben agreed to do all this. Six months later, the plan had failed in all aspects.

In elementary school, Ben had been diagnosed with ADD, but the medication he was given had such unpleasant side effects that, with the consent of his parents, he failed to take it regularly. When Ben returned home, his father took him for a brain scan at the Daniel G. Amen Clinic in Tacoma, Washington. The scan showed multiple areas in Ben's brain that were not functioning normally. The psychiatrist was able to prescribe medications better suited to Ben's unique brain. Unfortunately, Ben continued to be inconsistent in taking the medication and was angry when reminded to do so. Ben felt like he was being "treated like a child" and rebelled.

This illustrates one of the core dilemmas faced by families of adult gaming addicts. The addict is, developmentally, like a younger teenager, but the addict thinks of himself as an adult, demanding the privileges of adulthood without its responsibilities. From the parental point of view, this child is a chronological adult without adult maturity. It is extremely difficult for parents to figure out how to interact in a way that is helpful while taking care of their own needs and the needs of other children in the home.

At his wit's end, Ben's father sought help. Had there been an inpatient treatment center, Ben would have been referred there. Since there was not, the father was willing to structure the home to become a treatment environment. He was also able to hire his son to work for him in his business. He let Ben know that if the program was not followed adequately, Ben would have to leave. Here is what was required:

o   Ben was allowed no more computer time. If he wanted it badly enough, he could always go to the library.
o   Ben had to be working.
o   Ben was required to do specific chores at home such as mowing the lawn. These chores were clearly spelled out.

o   Ben had to attend regular therapy sessions to work on all his problems.

This story has a happy ending. For a period of time it looked as if Ben would not be able to rise to the occasion, and came close to being evicted. But because his father held the line with him, Ben is now working, slowly developing a social life in the real world, taking his medications, and starting to feel good about himself.

Often, we have found that adult children will go for counseling when confronted by their parents. This would be the best place to begin. A good format for expressing concerns is

Describe the situation (be brief and specific)
"You are gaming five or more hours a day, not working, and not doing well in school."

Express how you feel (start with "I"...)
"I am very concerned about you, and I'm angry. I feel taken advantage of."

Specify what you want
"You must stop gaming for a while, concentrate on your school work, and get counseling. And, we'd like you to talk with us about what is going on."

Spell out consequences (positive and/or negative)
"If you will agree to these things, then you can stay here. If not, you will have to make plans to leave by _____ ".

A *tough love* approach is terrifying for many parents who fear that their children will not survive outside the home. It takes both courage and love (along with a support group) to watch adult children flounder when you know how ill prepared they are to deal with real life. But how else are they going to learn? Our experience has been that once an adult child finds himself actually out of the home, parents are surprised at how resourceful they can be. These adult children find family, friends, or acquaintances with whom they can stay. Or, they quickly develop a willingness to play by their parents' rules. If you believe your child has some other condition, such as Asperger's syndrome that could render him truly unable to take care of himself, this is not a good option. Whatever your situation, we recommend you find a therapist to work with. The situation could get very difficult, and good support for the family is advised.

Ideally, you are reading this when your children are young, their brains and their habits are still highly malleable, and you can stop a serious problem from developing. If you are not in that advantageous position, however, and your child is an older teenager or an adult who has been gaming for many years, you would be wise to seek advice from a therapist who understands addictions and helps families cope with the problem. There are a small but growing number of therapists trained specifically to work with video game addiction. However, any therapist who understands that video gaming *can be* an addiction will be in a better position to help than a therapist who believes otherwise or has little experience with addiction treatment of any sort. Once you find a knowledgeable therapist, you can decide the best way to proceed.

Threats of Violence and Self-Harm

Occasionally, video game addicts will become violent or threaten violence when parents take drastic steps to stop their children from gaming — just like addicts who are deprived of their drugs. If this occurs, it lets you know that you are dealing with a serious addiction and you need professional help to cope with your situation. When violence occurs, a knife is drawn, or furniture is destroyed, call the police or a crisis hotline. You need protection and your child needs to experience the consequences of his or her actions. Your child could be having a psychotic break (if he has been on a gaming binge) and might need to be in the hospital. This is not the time to avoid embarrassment. Of course, do what needs to be done in the moment to stay safe from harm. But let this moment galvanize you into constructive action.

What Parents Can Do

The following bullet points summarize what parents can do regarding an adult child who has a problem with video gaming:

o   If your adult child will agree to it, have him or her evaluated to see if there are any other psychological problems that also need to be addressed (for example, Asperger's syndrome, bipolar disorder, ADD, or ADHD). If you know or strongly suspect that your child has Asperger's, be sure to follow the guidelines provided in Chapter 2. If your child is diagnosed as depressed, follow the guidance of the addiction therapist you are working with. Antidepressant medication is not automatically indicated when dealing with a depression that is related to an addiction.

o   If your adult child is uncooperative and unresponsive to your constructive confrontation and limit-setting, consider doing a formal intervention, as described in the next chapter. Interventions are designed to break through an addict's denial system, overwhelm them with loving messages that drive home the love and concern of family and friends, and open them to the possibility of receiving help.

o   Understand that your home may need to turn into a treatment facility of sorts. The rules and consequences (positive and negative) must be carefully thought through and enforced. You must decide such things as whether or not to have Internet access in your home during this period. Often, the wisest choice will be to *not* have it, giving your adult child a chance to abstain long enough to learn how to engage in real life. Some families have allowed limited access to the Internet with no video gaming and it has worked.

o   If you are allowing your adult child to stay in the home and he or she has agreed to live by your therapeutic rules, and you continue to have Internet access in your home, we suggest you install software that allows you to monitor what is happening on every computer in the home, including your child's laptop. This will be met with strong objection, but it may be the only way your child can be held accountable. Once it is installed, use it. Look for help to find appropriate software.

o   You must expect your adult child to shoulder adult responsibilities. This includes doing their fair share of chores, working and paying rent, or going to school (not taking classes on-line, but actually showing up in classrooms where they can socialize).

o   You would do well to attend regular meetings of Al-Anon Family Groups to get support from others who can relate to your family's problems. You may find information in the phone book or through an Internet search engine. Al-Anon is especially valuable if you plan to establish and follow through with tough but healthy boundaries.

o   Your adult child may need to attend both individual and group therapy. He or she can also be encouraged to attend a 12-step meeting. Since 12-step meetings for gamers does not yet exist in most places, Codependents Anonymous might be a reasonable starting point.

o   If all of this fails, you will be faced with even more difficult choices. You may serve your adult child best by not allowing him or her to live with you. We strongly recommend you get professional advice and support as you figure out what to do.

9
The Formal Intervention Option

A formal intervention is an option when parents find they have no effective parental authority with the gamer in the family. This usually seems to happen when the gamer reaches the age of seventeen or eighteen. Before then, we often find that if parents have good support and guidance, they can effectively reassert their authority and set appropriate limits with their teen. The older teen may respond well once parents learn how to set limits and mean it, particularly if affectionate bonds exist between the gamer and both parents.

Formal interventions (as opposed to poorly planned "confrontations" that often make problems worse) involve a trained therapist. The goal of an intervention is to break through an addict's *denial* system (all the rationalizations and delusions) with the intention of offering him or her little option but to see reality and the negative effects of addiction. The goal is to select a path toward health. Traditionally, interventions deal with *substance* addictions (alcohol, cocaine, etc.) but they can be used for *process* addictions (gambling, shopping, etc.) as well.

A trained, professional intervention specialist begins by preparing the family and friends who agree to be involved. There is more than one type of intervention, but the most common involves each person preparing exactly what he or she will *read* to the addict. This includes expressions of love and concern along with a list of negative impacts the addiction is having on the family. The intervention specialist is present, facilitating the whole thing. If all goes well (and most of the time it does), the addict accepts the help offered. If substance abuse is involved, the addict often agrees to go into a residential treatment program. Because there are, as yet, very few treatment programs that will take gaming addicts, the addict is asked to get help in other ways.

Emmit

Emmit was a teen who controlled his parents. They were too intimidated by him to be effective limit setters. He was eighteen when his mother contacted us. The family had moved from another state when Emmit was sixteen. Before the move, he had gotten along reasonably well with his parents and his younger brother. He had gamed, but not so much that it interfered with his school and social life. He was a normal, bright child. He did not want to move, and felt bitter toward his father for forcing the family to relocate.

Beginning with their arrival in their new home, Emmit fought with his father and brother, submerged himself into gaming, and refused to put effort into school. When the family arrived for counseling, Emmit was flunking out of his final high school semester. He refused to follow any of the limits and rules set by his parents, his participation in counseling was insincere, and he was increasingly hostile.

After considering all their options, the parents decided to go forward with a formal intervention. Family members flew in from out of state to participate. After much careful preparation, the day finally arrived. Emmit was unaware of what was about to take place. The loving confrontation of his family worked as planned and everyone was surprised to discover, beneath the hostile shell of this young man, the vulnerable boy they knew and loved. To the surprise of his parents, he agreed to go to Outward Bound for three weeks. This is called a *pattern interrupter*.

After twenty-one days away from the normal pattern of his life, he would have completed the most serious phase of withdrawal from his addiction (remember, his body had become addicted to his own neurochemistry in the form of dopamine) and he would be ready for a fresh start. On his return, he began individual and group therapy. For now, he is not allowed to play video games at all. His job is to reengage with life.

As long as he is cooperative at home and either works or returns to school, he is welcome to remain there. His parents are beginning their recovery as well. They participate in a support group for parents of gamers and attend family counseling with Emmit. Because he is now taking responsibility for himself, Emmit is able to work on his anger toward his father. Together, they are repairing their torn relationship.

Christopher

Christopher presents us with another story with a positive outcome. He was twenty-four when his parents contacted us. He was not living at home, but his parents were financially supporting him. He claimed to be attending community college, but was, in fact, failing because of a gaming addiction. His parents provided him an apartment, a car, and an allowance. They knew something had to be done, but did not know what.

After talking with a specialist, they decided to do a formal intervention. They had the resources to send him to a twenty-one-day outdoor adventure program. The success of his new, non-addicted self depended on him engaging life without gaming. This, they knew, would be a difficult thing because most of his friends gamed as well.

The intervention went well and Christopher, as did Emmit, agreed to spend three weeks in Outward Bound. When he returned, he participated in individual and group therapy on a weekly basis. He was clear with his friends that he could no longer game. Some of his friends dropped out of his life because they had nothing in common except the gaming. Others remained. Now busy with work and school, Christopher is doing well.

Evan

Evan is another young man for whom a formal intervention worked, but not as smoothly as with Emmit and Christopher. Evan grew up in a volatile family where his parents fought constantly. When he discovered Internet gaming at the age of fifteen, he became hooked immediately. It offered him an escape from the misery of his family life, was well suited to his ADD brain, and boosted his self-esteem within the narrow confines of the on-line gaming world.

His parents were so caught up in the disintegration of their marriage that they paid little attention to the boy who was gaming in the privacy of his bedroom. Both parents got mad at Evan for not doing his chores, but they rarely bothered him until they discovered he was flunking out of high school. By then it was too late. When they tried to take the computer out of his room, Evan ran screaming to the kitchen, grabbed a knife, and tried to attack his father. The parents were so scared that they put the computer back. When things calmed down, Evan told them not to worry because he would earn the credits he needed at the local community college. As Evan began college, his mother moved out. His gaming continued unabated and he failed all his courses.

Evan's parents contacted us for help. Like so many parents we meet, they were afraid of angering their son and were thus rendered impotent. Guilt also played heavily on their minds. They felt guilty for all the fighting they had done over the years, and understood that it contributed to their son's addiction. As they saw it, they felt guilty for taking away Evan's source of comfort and pleasure. Now the parents saw how much trouble their son was in and while they could not agree on much else, they did agree that Evan needed help. After considering their options, they chose to do a formal intervention.

Fortunately, the mother's grandparents lived nearby and they got along well with Evan. They participated in the decision to do an intervention. An intervention specialist worked with the parents, grandparents, family friends, and a younger brother. Intervention day came and everyone gathered at the house. Under some other pretext, Evan arrived there with his grandfather, only to find everyone gathered. He was angry, but stayed and listened. Giving nothing away emotionally, Evan agreed to the terms laid out for him if he were to continue living with his father. These terms included no gaming, no computer in his bedroom, working or going to school, going for counseling, and doing chores at home. If he failed these, he understood that he must move out. This family did not have the resources to send him away for a while (the *pattern interrupter* that can be so useful).

Very quickly Evan returned to his normal pattern. He sneaked a computer back into his room, neither worked nor attended school, and for a while it looked as if all the effort was a waste. It was not, however. Because Evan had signed an agreement which he was not living up to, his father finally summoned the courage to evict him from the house. Evan was shocked that his father had the strength to do it. He called his grandparents who agreed to let him come there, but only if the same agreements applied. Being healthier and stronger people, they made the agreements work. Evan never had his computer in their home, so his pattern of gaming was finally interrupted. He is now employed full time, contributing to the household, and feeling better about himself.

Disengaging from the Cyber world and engaging in real life is the challenge of all gaming addicts. It can be hugely difficult to make this transition. Remember, the brain of an addict of many years has been "rewired." Many developmental windows have closed, making it now quite difficult for the adult to learn the real-world skills that would have been relatively easy to learn as a younger person.

We do not yet know the extent to which their developmental delays can be mitigated. The old adage about brain neurons (if it's fired, it's wired) suggests that lots of practice is needed if these adults are to learn the life skills they need.

Decades of work with drug addicts and alcoholics has taught us that once addictive behaviors end, maturation restarts. Among those addicted to alcohol and other drugs, problems of various kinds may persist throughout life, depending on the degree to which their brains have suffered damage. This may also turn out to be true for the gaming addict, who might, for example, always have a brain that functions like an ADD brain, even when the genetic predisposition is not there. Eventually, research will tell us how well a game addict's brain can return to normal. Factors such as the age at which heavy gaming began and how many years it persisted will, undoubtedly, prove influential. Certainly it is good news that game addicts are not damaging their brains with chemicals that kill off brain cells. But the neural connections (the *neuronet*) that extensive gaming develops may have lasting and negative impacts.

Collin

Collin offers us a story that illustrates the profound and lasting impact of heavy gaming, and the dilemma parents face as they try to help. Collin's parents were from India. Collin was their only child and they had great expectations for him. Their rules were stringent, their expectations high, and they resorted to physical force if Collin was disobedient. The father was far harsher than the mother. Collin said he hated his father. He was allowed to game without limitations as long as grades stayed high and rules were followed.

Once Collin went off to college, he found the freedom intoxicating. Since he was furious with his father, he threw off his parents' expectations and indulged in gaming to his heart's content. By his second semester he had started to fail classes. He managed to hide his academic failure from his parents with a few tricks: he created a false grade report to show them, withdrew from classes by the withdrawal deadline, and enrolled in classes that he did not attend. The deception lasted until his mother got a letter from the university telling them they were kicking Collin out.

For the three years the deception lasted, Collin lived in shame and fear of discovery. To be found out was a relief and, yet, terrifying. He was profoundly depressed by this time and confided his suicidal thoughts to his mother. His father refused to speak to him. Fortunately, his mother found us and brought her son in for therapy. He knew he needed help and was completely cooperative.

Fifteen months later, Collin is doing well. He has been reinstated at the university and is again attending courses. He is struggling, but is not giving up. He often talks about how difficult it is for him to concentrate. His mind wanders and he constantly struggles to bring his attention back to the task at hand. And he longs to give up. He fantasizes about gaming and longs for escape from the arduous task of studying.

We see in Collin's story three consequences of his gaming: reduced self-discipline, reduced concentration, and reduced ability to memorize. In the gaming world, he constantly found immediate gratification. Over time, he lost the ability to delay gratification and tolerate hard, unpleasant, boring work. He describes will power and self-discipline as being like muscles that have gone flabby with disuse. He is trying to build them back up to the level he enjoyed as a high schooler, and he is finding it very difficult.

The same thing has happened to his ability to concentrate and memorize. As a teenager, when his gaming was not out of control, and had not gone on for so long, he had been good at both skills. After years of addictive gaming, he found these skills were severely compromised. The *neuronet* to support them was no longer there. The authors are optimistic that Collin will regain these lost skills and succeed in his college work. Collin, himself, is not so confident. At this writing, he has successfully completed his first term. He passed all his classes and is determined, but anxious.

Sex and the Internet

One last word about sex and the Internet. Children of any age, if allowed unmonitored, free access to the Internet, are likely to find (by design or by accident) pornography and other content of a sexual nature. This material abounds in Cyberspace. Some of it is found on professional sites, while much of it is amateur. Chat rooms and popular Websites that allow instant messaging, like Myspace.com, can easily lead to images from Webcams (video cameras attached to home computers) that are sexual in content. There are many teenagers and adults who are sending sexual images of themselves to friends and strangers. This sexual material is easy for children to access. So if you do not want your child exposed in this way, you must take steps to prevent it.

We have found that many parents are 1) unaware of what is on the Internet; 2) aware, but believe there is no way to stop their children from viewing these sights; or 3) believe that their child's exposure to sexual material is harmless. Let us begin with the third. Children can be harmed by inappropriate exposure to sexual material. Young children can be traumatized; teenagers can have their future sexual and romantic lives profoundly affected.

We assume that, as a parent, you want your child to one day enter into an intimate, committed partnership with someone he or she loves. This may be difficult to achieve if they carry traumatic feelings about sex or if they have come to dissociate sex from a loving relationship. A teenager is likely to be stimulated by sexual images or sex chat experienced on the Internet. Masturbation soon follows. When this is experienced again and again, sex for that teen comes to be associated not with the attractive youth next door (with whom they *could* have a healthy relationship) but with porn and sex chat. The natural steps that build toward emotional and sexual intimacy are missing. Those steps (flirting, dating, and courtship, etc.) are skills that teens must develop through practice with real, live people. On-line flirtations and Cyber sex are not good substitutes. Research in this area is limited, as yet, but the early research is showing that the more boys view pornography, the more they view sex as entertainment and women as objects.

The authors direct an outpatient treatment program for sex addicts. Universally, each sex addict has a history of early exposure to pornography, a disconnection between sex and love, and a fear of and confusion about emotional intimacy. We may not be able to shield our children from all inappropriate sexual material, but we can and should minimize it. Filters and monitoring software are appropriate and necessary if parents want to protect their children so they can develop normally.

Our experience with adult video game addicts is that most of them do not have a healthy sexuality or a healthy relationship to the opposite sex. Many heavy gamers have substituted an interest in *gaming* for an interest in *dating*. Their sex drive has largely gone underground. When they do feel it, they often handle their libido by looking for porn, quickly masturbating, and then returning to the more important business of gaming. What will happen if these gamers actually attempt to date? Will they be able to sustain both sexual and emotional intimacy? If their sexual template is primarily formed through Cyber sex and pornography, the outlook is not favorable unless hard work is done to change it. We know by the success of our program, which is 12-step based and immerses the addicts in a community of recovery, that positive change is possible. But how much better it would be if these folks had a healthy sexuality to begin with!

Let this be one more reason to do whatever it takes to help your children have a healthy relationship to the computer in general and video gaming in particular. As long as their time on the Internet is limited, the content is limited to what is appropriate, and they are supported in developing a healthy social life in the real world, their chances of entering into healthy, loving, sexually mature adult relationships are good.

Conclusion

We hope we have given you, in the pages of this book, enough information to make informed decisions about the role of video games in your family, and some idea of how to achieve this. We have explained what video game addiction is, how it develops, what you can do to prevent it, and how you can intervene if it has developed. We have given you information about possible harmful effects of video games on developing children, with chapters devoted to each major developmental stage in a child's life, along with ways to maintain an appropriate relationship to gaming technologies at each stage.

We have *not* given you specific information about software and hardware products that can assist you in setting and maintaining appropriate limits. These you must find for yourselves. There are now many places you can go for help. The library is a great place to start. Most librarians are well informed and able to help people in your position find this kind of information. There are books, journal articles, magazines, and numerous Websites that contain the information you may want about monitoring software, game reviews, the latest research on video games, etc. Be cautious as you read however (and this is where guidance from a librarian can be extremely valuable). Look for the research coming out of *independent* research institutions and universities, not from the game industry itself. With the information you have gained from this book we hope you will be able to read whatever you find with a critical eye.

We hope you will always keep in mind that good research takes a long time to be completed, written up, and reviewed. By contrast, the gaming industry is galloping ahead with its marketing teams. The pace of change is breathtaking. It's hard for the objective research to keep up. This is why it is crucial for you, the parents, to be cautious. The game industry is, for the most part, profit driven. It's a classic example of *buyer beware*.

Much as we might wish for it, we would be foolish to expect the gaming industry to go against their profit interests. It is reasonable for us to assume that profits will often trump ethics when there is a contest between them. We applaud those game developers who are committed to maintaining high ethical standards in the games they develop for entertainment and education. They exist, but they will flourish only if we, the consumers, buy only those games that we are confident will be beneficial to our children. We hope this book gives you the confidence you need to look for those games. You will need to carefully investigate each game you consider bringing into your home. It is such a powerful technology that it is worth taking the time to do this research. Your children need you to do it. We trust that you now understand why.

Bibliography

"AMA Takes Action on Video Games." American Medical Association. 27 June 2007. <http://www.ama-assn.org>.

Benoit, Marilyn. *The Dot.Com Kids and the Demise of Frustration Tolerance*. The Alliance for Childhood, 2005.

Brazelton, T. Berry. *Touchpoints: Birth to 3: Your Child's Emotional and Behavioral Development*. Da Capo Lifelong Books, 2006.

Bruner, Olivia and Kurt. *Playstation Nation: Protect Your Child from Video Game Addiction*. New York: Center Street, 2006.

Bushman, B, and C Anderson. "Violent Video Games and Hostile Expectations: a Test of the General Aggression Model." *Personality and Social Psychology Bulletin 28* (2002): 1679-1686.

Elkind, David. *The Hurried Child: 25th Anniversary Edition*. Da Capo Lifelong Books, 2006.

Elkind, David. *The Power of Play: Learning What Comes Naturally*. Da Capo Lifelong Books, 2008.

Elkins, Whitney L., Deborah A. Cohen, Lisa M. Koralewicz, and Stephanie N. Taylor. "After School Activities, Overweight, and Obesity among Inner City Youth." *Journal of Adolescence 27* (2004): 181-189.

Emotional and Behavioral Effects of Video Games and Internet Overuse. Council on Science and Public Health. American Medical Association, 2007.

Fair Play: Violence, Gender, and Race in Video Games. Children Now. 2001.

Gee, James Paul. *What Video Games Have To Teach Us About Learning and Literacy.* New York: Palgrave Macmillan, 2003.

Gentile, D. A., P. Lynch, J. Linder, and D. Walsh. "The Effects of Violent Video Game Habits on Adolescent Hostility, Aggressive Behaviors, and School Performance." *Journal of Adolescence 27* (2004): 5-22.

Gurian, Michael. *The Good Son: Shaping the Moral Development of Our Boys and Young Men.* New York: Putnam, 1999.

Healy, Jane. *Failure to Connect: How Computers Affect Our Children's Minds — And What We Can Do about It.* New York: Simon and Schuster, 1998.

Hernandez, Romel. "What to Make of Boys?" *Lewis and Clark Chronicle,* Summer 2007.

Koob, George F. and Moal, Michel Le. *Neurobiology of Addiction.* Oxford: Elsevier, 2006.

Koepp, M.J., Gunn, R.N., et al. "Evidence for Striatal Dopamine Release During a Video Game." *Nature, 393,* (1998).

Lewis, Thomas, Amini, Fari, and Lannon, Richard. *A General Theory of Love.* New York: Random House, 2001.

Lowenstein, Doug. *Interview with Atari.* WomenGamers.Com. Mar. 2000. 25 Nov. 2007 <http://www.womengamers.com/forums/viewtopic.php?t=5622>.

"Media Violence Facts and Statistics (Printable Version)." *The Surgeon General of the United States. The Television Violence Monitoring*

Project. 15 Jan. 2008 <http://www.safeyouth.org/scripts/faq/mediaviolstats.asp>.

Marble, Colleen. "Log on to Safety." *American Academy of Pediatrics.* Summer 2007. 15 Jan. 2008 <http://www.aap.org/family/healthychildren/07summer/internetsafety.pdf>.

National Health and Nutrition Examination Survey. Centers for Disease Control and Prevention. Maryland: U.S. Department of Health and Human Services, 2006. Fall 2007 <www.cdc.gov/nchs/nhanes.htm>.

Ramsey, Evan. *Interview with Anderson Cooper.* Anderson Cooper 360 Degrees. CNN. CNN. 25 Apr. 2006.

"Resources for Parents & Guardians." The National Center for Missing & Exploited Children. Jan. 2008. Autumn 2007 <www.missingkids.com>.

Rideout, Victoria, and Elizabeth Hamel. "The Media Family: Electronic Entertainment in the Lives of Infants, Toddlers, Preschoolers, and Their Parents." Kaiser Family Foundation. May 2006. Winter 2007 <www.kff.org>.

Rideout, Victoria. "Parents, Children and Media: a Kasier Family Foundation Survey." Kaiser Family Foundation. June 2007. 14 Jan. 2008 <www.kff.org>.

Roberts, Donald, Ulla G. Foehr, and Victoria Rideout. "Generation M: Media in the Lives of 8 - 18 Year Olds." Kaiser Family Foundation. Mar. 2005. Stanford University. 14 Jan. 2008 <www.kff.org>.

Seidman Milburn, Sharon, Dana R. Carney, and Aaron M. Ramirez. "Even in Modern Media, the Picture is Still the Same: a Content Analysis of Clipart Images — Statistical Data Included." *Sex Roles: a Journal of Research* (2001).

"Sleep for All Ages." National Sleep Foundation. 15 Jan. 2008 <http://www.sleepfoundation.org/site/c.huIXKjM0IxF/b.2417429/k.BD15/Sleep_for_All_Ages.htm>.

DeAngelis, Tory. "Web Pornography's Effects on Children". *APA Monitor on Psychology. 38*, No. 10 (2007).

Youth Violence: a Report of the Surgeon General. U.S. Department of Health and Human Services. 2001

Zimmerman, Frederick J., Dimitri A. Christakis, and Andrew N. Meltzoff. "Associations between Media Viewing and Language Development in Children under Age 2 Years." *The Journal of Pediatrics 151* (2007): 364-368.

Gaming Glossary

Gaming Platforms

consoles: Currently this mainly refers to the XBox, PlayStation, and Nintendo Game Cube/Wii systems. Console games have a long history in the home. Over the last twenty plus years, console games, along with most technologies, have increased in sophistication and in the number of applications. Brand names such as Atari, Nintendo, NES, etc., have come and gone. Consoles are no longer constrained to the play of arcade-style games; they now have the ability to access the Internet, play DVDs, and are in some ways as powerful as personal computers.

hand-held games: Hand-held games have also been in the marketplace for quite a while and are becoming increasingly more sophisticated. The old Mattel handheld football game that included simple, small red-lighted dots and dashes has given way to fairly advanced games with graphics unheard of even ten years ago. At the time of this writing, console games include not only such systems as Nintendo Game Boy but games that can be played on wireless services such as your mobile phone.

personal computers (PC's): Traditionally, PCs have been the platform of choice for gamers who play the types of games that require more horsepower than the console games of the past. Over the years, console platforms have become so advanced that this gulf has narrowed quite a bit. However, PCs are generally used in favor of consoles for games that require high amounts of computing resources such as World of Warcraft and other MMORPGs (massive multiplayer online role-playing games).

Games/Genres

Listed below are some of the general types of gaming genres and examples of some of the games that would typically fit that genre. Keep in mind that there are many different gaming styles and that the gaming industry itself is constantly evolving and developing new types of games. Not all games fit into any one of the traditional styles or genres and there are no hard and fast rules or definitions of the genres themselves.

arcade games: These games are similar to the coin-operated arcade games such as Pacman, Space Invaders, etc.

fighting games: This is another genre that has been popularly played for many years. The Mortal Kombat series is one of the most recognizable, but with the advent of Nintendo's Wii platform, the player can now play fighting games using hand-held devices that simulate actual punching.

first-person shooter (FPS): First-person shooters have become wildly popular over the last fifteen years. An FPS gives the gamer the point of view of the person holding the shotgun, ray gun, sniper rifle, or whichever weapon is applicable for the game. First-person shooters have a wide variety of environments, the most popular of which are

Outer-Space (the Halo series), World War 2 (Call of Duty, Medal of Honor, Battlefield 1942) or fantasy (Doom, Duke Nukem, and Quake).

MMORPGs (massively multiplayer on-line RPGs): See also RPGs. MMORPGs refer to role playing games that take place on-line and can have thousands of people playing at any one time. In addition to Everquest and World of Warcraft, some of the popular MMORPG titles include Lord of the Rings and City of Heroes.

puzzle games/adventure games: This genre includes such titles as MYST where the player explores a fantasy world trying to solve puzzles and find the answers posed to them in the storyline of the game.

real-time strategy (RTS): An RTS is a strategy game where decisions are made in real time. For example, if one is playing "Command and Conquer," the player and his enemies build a home base, train soldiers, and explore territory — at the same time. These types of games can be played against the computer or against one or more on-line opponents. Other examples of these games include Age of Empires and Dune. Pausing these games is not a problem when playing against a computer because the computer stops, too. When other people are involved, they can continue playing and gain large advantages over the player who pauses. See role-playing games and MMORPGs.

role playing games (RPGs): Role playing games are where the gamer takes on the role of a fantasy or fictional character. Dungeons and Dragons is probably one of the more famous of the early RPGs but they have evolved into more complex games such as Everquest and World of Warcraft.

simulation games (SIMs): These are games that simulate some type of real-life or fantasy world. One can get into an airplane and simulate being a pilot or can create their own neighborhoods and people who live in them. Examples of these types of games include, Flight Simulator and The Sims. The next generation of simulation games includes such titles as Guitar Hero, Rock Band, and Dance Dance Revolution. These particular games involve a lot of hands-on play. Some require following dance steps and or singing, while others have the gamer simulating playing an instrument.

sports games: Sports games have maintained popularity over the years and include several titles that are anxiously looked forward to each year. They can be played both as a single player experience and on-line. Good examples are Madden Football and Tiger Woods' Golf. They also include numerous auto racing games and games for almost any sport imaginable.

turn-based strategy: Turn-based strategy games are played with the players taking turns, as in chess. There is less pressure to act quickly in these games than in RTS games because the opponent is not making moves while the player who has the current turn is deciding what to do.

Gaming Terminology

Below is a short list of some of the more widely used gaming words and terms.

Please keep in mind that there are literally thousands of terms used within the gaming community including some that are unique to the style of game being played. For example, some of the terms used in a first-person shooter might not be used in a real-time strategy game.

In addition, some words and terms are similar or exactly the same as the popular terms used by people when sending text messages over their cell phone. For example the popular instant message "LOL" for "Laugh out Loud" is also commonly used during on-line game play. As a parent, if you run across a word or term you do not understand or see on this list, it should be fairly easy to do an Internet search to locate it and find a definition.

aggro: Aggression, monster aggression, or the amount of monster aggression directed toward a player. Often also referred to as "hate."

avatar: A Hindu term commonly used on-line to describe the users' representation of themselves seen on the computer screen, generally as a 2D image.

boss: A powerful enemy in a game that must be fought and overcome for players to advance or earn points in a game.

camp: To sit in one place for long periods of time killing monsters or waiting in ambush.

clan: Similar to a club or guild. Clans are generally for avid gamers that join together to achieve similar gaming goals.

crafting: Many games, especially MMORPGs, give the players abilities to craft or create items, such as Weaponsmith.

ding: To gain a higher level of experience.

farm: Farming is when a player spends time gathering resources, usually to sell or to use in crafting.

flame war: interactions between a set of Internet users characterized by hostility, insults, and a general lack of concern for social conventions, usually about an issue where strong feelings exist, but no general agreement about preferences (e.g., are PCs or Macs better?).

flaming: hostile and insulting interactions between Internet users.

frag: Usually used when something or someone is blown up.

gamespeak: A voice-over Internet application that enables a player playing certain games to use a headset to speak with other players on-line.

goldfarming: A common activity where people actively play the game specifically to make virtual gold or platinum but then turn around and sell it on-line for actual money. For some, this is a business.

grinding: Usually used to describe game play that is slow and methodical. The term is used when someone is trying to get to a higher level or when farming for items.

grouping: When multiple players band together as a team during game play.

guild: The group formed by multiple players (a clan or team) to achieve a shared gaming goal.

hacker: A hack or hacker is usually associated with a cheat or someone who is cheating.

loot: When a monster or other player has been killed, generally a player can loot the body for items.

leet, elite, leetspeak: Referring to savvy gamers who generally use alphanumeric characters to spell words, e.g., "l33tspeak".

level up: Increase skill and power by getting a character to a higher level. Characters start at level one and increase their level as they kill enemies, learn new skills, etc.

LFG (Looking for Group): Usually, a setting to indicate that a person is looking to join with others.

LMAO: Laugh My Ass Off.

LOL: Laugh Out Loud.

newbie (newb, n00b, noob): Referring to someone new to the game and/or playing like someone new to the game. Generally used as an insult.

mod or modding: Many games allow and encourage users at home to make their own changes to the game itself. These are called Mods and are relatively easy to do. Examples of Mods can be something as small as a new uniform on a soldier to something as sophisticated as a new world or playing zone which can be loaded and played on-line by others.

NPC: Non-Player Character. Computer generated character in the game, not controlled by a person.

OOC: Out of Character. (When someone is communicating in-game but out of their character.)

owned (also pwnd): Primarily used in the gaming community as a description of domination. Either being dominated or dominating someone else. "I pwnd you." Or, "I just got owned." Often used as an insult. "Prepare to be pwnd."

pet: Many RPGs and MMORPGs include the ability to own or create a pet through incantations or spells.

plat: Platinum

POS (Parent over shoulder): meaning the gamer can't talk freely because a parent is watching.

PvP: Player vs. Player. Usually described when players can attack and kill one another in-game.

pwn, pwnd: See *owned*.

spam: Usually referring to a message that is unimportant or annoying to other players.

tell: Sending someone a "tell." A private message specific to another player in the game.

toon: Reference to a player's gaming character. Based on the word *cartoon*.

raid: When a large number of people and/or groups get together to kill a common enemy or enemies.

ROFL: Roll on the Floor Laughing.

ventrilo: A brand of Voice-over Internet (VoI) software. See *gamespeak* above.

WTF: What the F---.

Index

About the Authors

Hilarie Cash, PhD, LMHC

Hilarie is the co-founder of Internet/Computer Addiction Services and has a private practice in Redmond, WA. She has assisted Jay Parker in developing the No More Secrets Program for sex and love addicts, and has spearheaded the creation of the Gaming and Internet Treatment Program. She is a speaker, teacher, and author and has appeared, among other places, on ABC News, CNN, NPR, PBS, the BBC, and in print in the *Seattle Times*, *USA Today*, *U.S. News and World Report*, and the *New York Times*.

Kim McDaniel, MA, LHMC

Kim McDaniel is a devoted parent and wife, and has been a professional counselor for the past nineteen years. She is a Licensed Mental Health Counselor with a BA degree in psychology from California State University, Northridge and an MA degree from Pepperdine University. She has provided clinical services to children and adolescents at several residential and hospital facilities. Presently, Mrs. McDaniel's practice is focused on providing psychological services to families, adolescents, and children.